# DON'T GIVE UP
# DON'T GIVE IN

# DON'T GIVE UP
# DON'T GIVE IN

## LIFE LESSONS FROM
## AN EXTRAORDINARY MAN

# LOUIS ZAMPERINI
## AND DAVID RENSIN

piatkus

PIATKUS

First published in the US in 2014 by Dey St., an imprint of
William Morrow Publishers,
a division of HarperCollins Publishers

First published in Great Britain in 2014 by Piatkus
This paperback edition published in 2015 by Piatkus

13 5 7 9 10 8 6 4 2

A CIP catalogue record for this book
is available from the British Library.

ISBN 978-0-349-40647-3

Printed and bound in Great Britain by
Clays Ltd, St Ives plc

Papers used by Piatkus are from well-managed forests
and other responsible sources.

MIX
Paper from
responsible sources
FSC® C104740

Piatkus
An imprint of
Little, Brown Book Group
100 Victoria Embankment
London EC4Y 0DY

An Hachette UK Company
www.hachette.co.uk

www.littlebrown.co.uk

FOR MY LATE WIFE, CYNTHIA;
MY CHILDREN, CISSY AND LUKE;
AND MY GRANDSON, CLAYTON

# Contents

*People tell me, "You're such an optimist." Am I an optimist? An optimist says the glass is half full. A pessimist says the glass is half empty. A survivalist is practical. He says, "Call it what you want, but just fill the glass."*

*I believe in filling the glass.*

—Louis Silvie Zamperini

# Coauthor's Note

When I learned that Louie Zamperini had died on July 2, 2014, I didn't want to believe that he was gone. Impossible. Inconceivable. Just two days earlier we had sent the manuscript for this book to our editors, and I looked forward to us celebrating its publication. But sadly, death comes for us all—even for those like Louie who deserve to live forever.

Louie's family issued this statement: "After a forty-day-long battle for his life, he peacefully passed away in the presence of his entire family, leaving behind a legacy that has touched so many lives. His indomitable courage and fighting spirit were never more apparent than in these last days."

"We're all a little afraid of death," Louie had said the last time we'd met, when we broached the subject of mortality. "We're afraid because no matter how old you are you're always making plans and you don't want to be interrupted. I'm ninety-seven years old, but after everything that's happened in my life,

I feel as if I've lived two hundred years—and I wouldn't mind two hundred more so that I can keep doing what I've been doing."

What he'd been doing, he explained, "was helping the underdog. That's been my program. That's been my whole life."

———

SINCE COLLABORATING WITH Louie on his 2003 autobiography, *Devil at My Heels*, we'd become friends. When we spoke—or had a meal when he had the time; Louie was always going somewhere, doing something (age did not seem to affect him)—he would talk nonstop, regaling me with stories of his latest adventures, travels, and appearances. I'd hear about celebrities he'd met (who were as impressed with him as he was with them), fan letters he'd received, people he'd helped, and impromptu tales from his life after the war. He'd tell me about *Unbroken* author Laura Hillenbrand's latest research discovery. He'd ask about my wife and son, give parenting advice, and talk proudly about his family.

Every now and then my phone would ring and there would be Louie, who, without much preamble, would launch into new thoughts for this book while I scrambled to turn on the tape recorder. We'd begun sketching out *Don't Give Up, Don't Give In* after *Devil at My Heels* was published. At the time, it was called *All Things Work Together for Good*, which was a bedrock aspect of Louie's attitude toward life.

But *Unbroken* had come along, and with it in the works Louie really had no time to spare, so we decided to put our next project on the back burner. In the meantime, because he'd occasionally kvetch about how busy he was, I loved to tease him about what I promised would be the reaction to *Unbroken*, and all the attention he'd get. "If you think you're busy now, just wait," I told a man who had already been a huge public figure for most of his life.

In December 2013, Louie's daughter, Cynthia, called with some news. "My dad says he still has stories he wants to tell." Was I interested in reviving our book?

I immediately said yes. I cleared my schedule and we met weekly to work on what we now titled, *Don't Give Up, Don't Give In*. Unlike our first collaboration, our sessions couldn't go on for hours. Louie was, after all, ninety-seven. But age had not diminished his always unflagging enthusiasm. And his mind was clear. So we sat in his home office, looking at the broad sweep of Hollywood and downtown Los Angeles through the picture window, he wearing his University of Southern California cap and blue jacket, and me pushing the digital recorder closer and closer to make sure I got every word.

Once, when I arrived for our usual 10 a.m. appointment, Louie answered the door.

"Oh, no!" he said. "It's you." This was not his usual greeting. I discovered I had been mistakenly left off the schedule.

"Are you okay?" I said. He looked a bit worn out.

"I just woke up," he said. "Tom Brokaw was here yesterday interviewing me, and they had to put cardboard all over the floor for the equipment, and there were so many people, and . . . I'm a little exhausted."

"Let's just reschedule," I said.

"No, no. Come on in. I can talk for half an hour, okay?"

Typical Louie, he got more loquacious as he reminisced with relish about both a sailing trip along the Mexican Baja coast during which he'd gone missing and a pesky parrot named Hogan. He loved Hogan. "Make sure Hogan is in the book," he reminded me, when I finally said goodbye an hour and a half later.

Of course, this book wasn't Louie's only project. *Unbroken* had become a film, directed by Angelina Jolie, and he'd promised to be available to help however he could to support and promote it. And then there was his daily life: meals with the family, reading the never-ending fan mail and requests for photos and autographs, figuring out ways to help kids in need (a habit for sixty-five years), and looking forward to when Angelina would come to visit, often bearing gifts.

"He was my friend, my mentor, my hero," she said after Louie's passing, "It is a loss impossible to describe. We are all so grateful for how enriched our lives are for having known him. We will miss him terribly."

Like so many others, I cherished my time with Louie. I

marveled at his cheerfulness, open heart, self-awareness, and stunning ability to forgive. He was the content of his character and an example to us all. And yet, I know that I am not alone in finding it almost impossible to explain Louie's essence, to articulate exactly what made Louie who he was. Why was he so special? Did he even know? The answer now remains just out of reach.

In the end I guess that's how it should be, leaving us all the more about which to ponder and reflect, and to miss about him always.

—DAVID RENSIN, JULY 2014

# Introduction

F. Scott Fitzgerald once wrote that "there are no second acts in American lives."

I don't believe that. How could I?

I'm ninety-seven and I've done and been through so much that I feel as if I've lived for two hundred years. My mind is still sharp, my spirit is full, and I haven't lost my zest for life.

Some of you know my story because you've read my 2003 autobiography, *Devil at My Heels*. Or you've read about me in Laura Hillenbrand's 2010 bestselling biography, *Unbroken*, which has become a movie directed by Angelina Jolie. Maybe you were in the audience when I spoke at your school, church, hospital, or organization. Perhaps you saw me run with an Olympic torch, or watched me being interviewed on television, or discovered my war exploits in a magazine or newspaper. Did you spend a week at my Victory Boys Camp? I've given talks on cruise ships, and to the military. Did I counsel you or a member of your family when the need arose, or was I seated at the table next to yours at El Cholo, my favorite Mexican restaurant in Los Angeles?

I've done a lot, so anything is possible.

As a kid growing up in Torrance, California, in the 1920s and 1930s, I made more than my share of trouble for my parents and the neighborhood, and mostly got away with it. But at 15, thanks to my older brother, Pete, I turned my life around. Just in the nick of time he showed me how to channel my skill for running away from the police into a talent for racing around a high school track—and after a brief rough start, I took to it as if I'd been thrown a life preserver. In 1934, when I was 17, I set the high school interscholastic world record for the mile of 4:21.2, at the prelims for the California State Championships.

After graduating from high school in 1936, I made the U.S. Olympic team for the 5000-meter race by running to a dead heat for first place with Don Lash in the trials. I only placed eighth in Berlin against other great runners—Lash came in 13th—but I was the first of my team across the finish line. Hitler noticed my 56-second final lap and asked to meet me. "Ah, you're the boy with the fast finish," he said. And that was that.

I attended the University of Southern California between 1936 and 1940, and ran with a passion. I set the National Collegiate Athletic Association mile record in 1938 at the championship meet in Minneapolis. My time of 4:08.3 stood for fifteen years. In 1939, I ran a few seconds slower, but won the mile race again. My goal was to be the first to break the four-minute mile barrier at the 1940 Tokyo Olympics, and the consensus was that I had an excellent chance. But World War II got in the way. I was heartbroken.

I got a job at Lockheed Corporation in Burbank. During lunch, I'd watch one P-38 after another fly in and out of the company airfield. That seemed exciting so I applied to the Army Air Corps to be a pilot, but washed out of flight school because I couldn't take spinning in the air. Instead I became a bombardier, stationed in Hawaii. I flew in many hair-raising raids throughout the Pacific theater, including narrowly escaping death when our B-24 bomber, nicknamed *Superman*, was all shot up in a raid on the island of Nauru.

On May 27, 1943, while on a rescue mission near Palmyra Atoll, eight hundred miles south of the Hawaiian Islands, the beaten-up B-24 we had to use at the last minute—it no longer flew combat missions—blew an engine as we scanned the ocean at eight hundred feet. We crashed into the Pacific. I was trapped in the fuselage and going down. I thought I was a goner.

Miraculously, I survived. When I surfaced I saw that the pilot, Phil (Russell Phillips), and tail gunner, Mac (Francis McNamara), were alive too. The ocean was on fire and our other eight crewmen were gone. I managed to snag two life rafts, gave Phil first aid for a serious head gash, and then settled in to wait for our boys to find us.

No one did.

The tail gunner panicked the first night and ate all the enriched chocolate rations while Phil and I slept. Now we had nothing. Days passed. We survived on the occasional—raw—albatross that landed on the raft and the few fish that the sharks didn't get first, and caught a couple of small sharks and feasted on their livers. We had little protection from the sun and, after our limited water ration ran out, fresh water only when it rained. But we did have one advantage: our minds. Thanks to the mental discipline I'd developed as a world-class athlete, and the wisdom I'd absorbed from a wise physiology professor at USC, I was able to keep sharp and help Phil do the same.

On the twenty-seventh day we saw a plane. Rescue? No, a Japanese fighter. It strafed us again and again. We slipped into the water to avoid the bullets, and kept an eye out for sharks—and a fist ready to punch their snouts if they came too close. We escaped injury but the rafts were riddled with holes and needed serious pumping and patching while the sharks circled. Then a great white shark began to hunt us.

After thirty-three days Mac died. We buried him at sea. Phil and I hung on.

By then I had begun to do what everyone in a real or metaphorical foxhole does: I desperately asked God to intervene, saying, "I promise to seek you and serve you if you just let me live."

By the forty-sixth day we'd drifted nearly two thousand miles west to the Marshall Islands. After surviving a huge storm, we were rescued on the forty-seventh day—emaciated and near death—by the Japanese.

Initially they were decent, but that quickly devolved into two and a half years of torture and humiliation at numerous prison camps, much of it doled out by Sergeant Mutsuhiro Watanabe, a psychopathic and vindictive prison guard nicknamed the Bird. He thought that if he beat me enough I'd make propaganda broadcasts for the Japanese. I never did.

When the war ended, Phil and I were still alive and made it home. The press called me a hero. To me, heroes are guys with missing arms or legs—or lives—and the families they've left behind. There were so many. But because I was an Olympian and a sports celebrity with an incredible story—including having been declared dead by the Army—I got lots of attention. I can't say I didn't like it.

What I *didn't* like was that I couldn't find my place in the world and had what we now call post-traumatic stress disorder (PTSD). To compensate for growing frustration and a desire to take revenge for the misery I'd been through, I drank too much, got into fights, had an inflated ego, and no self-esteem. I also had constant nightmares about killing the Bird.

Somehow I managed to hold it together enough to meet and marry the girl of my dreams, Cynthia Applewhite. But I was caught in a relentless personal downward spiral, and almost lost her, my family, and my friends before I hit bottom, looked up—literally and figuratively—and found faith in 1949, in a tent on a Los Angeles street corner, listening to a young preacher named Billy Graham. The drink went down the drain. No more smoking. No more fighting. And I never dreamed of the Bird again.

But deciding to devote your life to God, whatever your religion, doesn't mean instantaneous, nonstop happiness. Hard work lay ahead. I fought despondency and doubt, and tried to come to terms with what had happened to me after years of taking life for granted.

My faith grew. A year later I returned to Japan. I asked to meet my prison guards—now incarcerated as war criminals— determined to forgive them all in person. The hardest thing in life is to forgive. But hate is self-destructive. If you hate somebody you're not hurting the person you hate, you're hurting yourself. Forgiveness is healing.

I wanted to forgive the Bird, too, but he was listed as missing, possibly a suicide.

When I returned home, I remembered the promise I'd made on the raft. I'd finally sought Him. Now I was determined to serve Him—and I did. For more than sixty-five years, I've devoted myself to a life of service and of sharing my story.

I have never ceased to be amazed at the response.

————

I'M OFTEN ASKED if, given the chance, I'd live my life the same way again. I have wondered about that as well—for about five seconds. When I think of the juvenile delinquency, injuries, torture, and many near-death experiences, the answer is a definite no. That would be crazy.

Of course, enduring and surviving those challenges led to many years of positive influence which helped neutralize the catastrophes and eventually delivered great rewards. I've been honored and blessed with impossible adventures and opportunities, a wonderful family, friends, and fans all over the world. That I'd gladly repeat.

It's obvious that one part of the story can't happen without the other.

And so I accept it. I am content.

————

YOU'D THINK THAT all that's happened to me would be plenty for one life, but unlike General MacArthur, this old soldier would not simply fade away.

In 1956, a publisher asked me to write an autobiography. I called it *Devil at My Heels*. We did it quickly and I wasn't crazy about it, but Universal Pictures bought the rights for Tony Curtis to play me. He made *Spartacus* instead, and my movie never happened. I didn't mind.

At the same time, I started an outreach camp program for boys who were as wayward as—or worse than—I had been. Victory Boys Camp was Outward Bound before Outward Bound. Thousands of boys got the counseling and fresh start they needed, and I would eventually help establish similar programs in England, Germany, and Australia.

As a wartime "hero" with a compelling story that I made my mission to share, I also made friends with Hollywood royalty, Los Angeles business bigwigs, sports figures, politicians, and even a noir era gangster or two. I climbed a glacier and almost died, and managed to run into trouble at sea again. Twice.

Mostly, though, I settled into a comfortable life as a veteran, Olympian, and man of faith. With my wife, Cynthia, an author and an artist with an irrepressible zest for living, I raised two wonderful children, Cissy and Luke. I was happy.

———

THINGS CHANGE. IN 1997, I was "rediscovered" by CBS Sports. They were looking for stories to tell on their broadcast of the 1998 Winter Olympics at Nagano, Japan, which was very near to my last prison camp during the war. They were surprised to find me alive. My story, produced by Draggan Mihailovich and reported by Bob Simon, aired on the night of the closing ceremonies. The next year it was repeated on *48 Hours*. I got the chance to completely rewrite and update *Devil at My Heels* the way I thought it should have been done in the first place. The result shared very little with the original book—except the title. The movie interest started again. We got closer, but it didn't happen. I didn't mind.

Just before *Devil at My Heels* was published in 2003, author Laura Hillenbrand wrote to ask if she could write my biography. I was flattered. I had read her marvelous book, *Seabiscuit*. But I said no: I'd just finished my own book.

Laura didn't give up, she didn't give in. She kept calling and eventually convinced (charmed?) me into changing my mind. I'm glad I did. Seven years and hundreds of hours of interviews later (plus her in-depth research that told me more about my life than even I knew), her book, *Unbroken*, came out in 2010, and has been on the *New York Times* and other bestseller lists ever since. Then the movies called again, and this time it happened, with Angelina Jolie directing. A phenomenal woman, one in a million, with her whole heart in the project.

What does it all mean? One of my favorite Bible verses has the answer: "All things work together for good."

———

SOON AFTER *Devil at My Heels* went to press in 2003, my co-author, David Rensin, and I began work on a little follow-up. My life hadn't ended with the war, or when I became a Christian. In fact, my most important life's work had just begun: helping kids, telling my story, inspiring a positive attitude in others. As a result, I was overwhelmed with mail thanking me and, often, asking me for advice. I kept the letters for the longest time, making thick notebook binders, but because I couldn't begin to answer them all, I decided that I might instead share a few stories and see if there were any universal lessons I could draw from my entire life—before, during, and after World War II.

But I had also begun to help Laura with *Unbroken* and there just weren't enough hours in the day. David and I put our book—this book—on hold until we could come back to it.

We had to wait ten years, but I finally found the time to do that.

Whether at a book signing, a friendly meal, a public appearance, talking to the press, or in casual encounters, I'm inevitably asked three questions:

1. What did you do after the war?
2. What's your secret for a good life?
3. How does your faith play a role?

*Don't Give Up, Don't Give In* is my answer to those questions. The answers aren't always simple but they have reoccurred throughout my life.

What I hope you'll discover is that I'm just an ordinary man with faults who, when confronted with extraordinary circumstances—in sports, in war, in life, and in faith—resolved to not give up and not give in, to keep looking for answers, and to make my life count right up to the last minute. I'm just a grateful survivor who realized I had something to give and became devoted to setting an example for others by being prepared, by having the proper attitude, and by trying to inspire.

It wasn't easy. Sometimes I just got lucky. But I gave it a try. You can, too, in your own way, whatever your goal in life.

Enjoy. And thank you.

LOUIS ZAMPERINI, HOLLYWOOD, CALIFORNIA, JULY 2014

# Run for Your Life

*Running at USC, 1938, the year*
*Louis set the NCAA mile record of 4:08:03.*

# The Family Rules

My father had a rule: We pay our bills first, and then we eat.

We all need a code of ethics to guide us, especially in tough times when everyone has to do their part for the greater good, for the family or the group to survive.

We lived on Gramercy Avenue in Torrance, California. In the 1920s and 1930s it was a small industrial town on the outskirts south of Los Angeles. There were more fields than houses and the barley rose three feet tall.

The open land was full of rabbits, ducks, mud hens, and, in the ocean, abalone—the poor man's food. If we were short on money, I had to go out and shoot or catch something for dinner. It was a good lesson for all of us: pitch in and help. Everyone in the family knew that to survive we had to make sacrifices.

I had odd jobs that earned me a nickel here, a dime there. If I went with the ice man all day, I got fifty cents for the eight hours. I churned butter at the dairy to make a dime. I gave it all to my mother so she could finish out the week with food until my dad got paid. A dime went a long way. When we could afford it, we took great joy in buying something from the ice cream sherbet man, who pushed his cart down every street in town. My favorite flavor was grape.

My mother was strict, but she was fair. She worked hard and taught her children essential values in the process. Every morning before school we had a chore to do—so we got used to participating and working when we were young.

My mother was also a fabulous cook. When times improved she served more than one main dish at dinner. Everybody ate. Everybody was cheerful. After dinner we'd walk around the block and talk among ourselves and with neighbors. We played music: my mother on the violin, my father on the guitar and mandolin. My mother's brother Louis could play just about anything. He was in the orchestra on the *Lurline*, the cruise ship that journeyed between Los Angeles and Honolulu. Neither my older brother, Pete, nor I played an instrument, but we sang.

Sometimes, when we ran out of money, Pete and I headed for the beach—but not to fish. I'd made a sifter out of quarter-inch screen. We ran it through the sand hoping to find small change. We swept under the monkey bars at our grade school—maybe some kid had lost his lunch money—and then we scoured the high school lot. If we were lucky we might pick up as much as fifty cents.

Of course, we didn't keep any of it for ourselves. That would have been against the family rules of all for one and one for all.

# Anyone Can Turn
# Their Life Around

———

I was a rotten kid.

It's true. Sure, I helped out at home, but I was restless and mischievous (and worse), and my behavior upset my family and eventually forced me to make one of the most important choices of my life.

I was always in trouble: with my father and mother, with the neighborhood, with the school, and with the police—when they could catch me. I had wonderful parents, good sisters, and a great brother who always wanted to help me go straight. Yet I still tried to find ways to get in trouble, mainly to see if I could get away with it. I used to blame it on having an itch for adventure. I wanted to try everything.

Looking back, I realize I also had a big problem with self-esteem.

When I was very young, I couldn't speak English. Even though I was born in America, my parents spoke Italian at home, and so did I. I was held back in first grade because I couldn't understand my teacher. My English was so broken that my teacher told my folks that they *had* to speak English at home in order to help me. What's funny is that now, years later, I've forgotten how to speak Italian.

Because I spoke so poorly, I was picked on. I dreaded recess. The other kids surrounded me, taunted me, jeered, kicked, and punched me until, out of pure frustration, I spewed a stream of Italian swear words. They seemed very entertained.

I thought I was ugly. I hated my legs, big ears, and especially my hair. It was black and wiry and I wished it were straighter. I combed it back but it wouldn't stay. I wet it down at night, pushed it into shape, and slept with a nylon or silk stocking on my head. Didn't work.

Because I spent so much time trying to get my hair to behave and look like the other guys', if anybody touched a single strand they were in trouble. Once, I even hit a girl who did—though I didn't know she was a girl. I just felt the touch and turned and swung without looking. Fortunately, the blow was only glancing.

My older brother, Pete, could have teased me; instead he tried to help me. He thought that wearing the stocking at night was a great idea. We also experimented with different ways to grease my hair back—including olive oil. (Later, in the deepest part of my antisocialness, I chewed raw garlic to keep the kids away. I guess all I was missing were stewed tomatoes, spices, and a saucepan.)

School fights were common, and I was usually on the losing end. My dad, who worked as a bench machinist for the Pacific Electric Railroad, made me a set of weights out of lead and taught me how to box. Got me a punching bag. I took to it like a starving man, and soon, when I was teased, I fought back. Viciously. And won.

———

I STARTED SMOKING when I was six years old. In those days many of the adults we were supposed to look up to smoked, so it makes sense that I was curious.

I remember the first time. I was walking to school when somebody tossed a lit cigarette butt out of their car window. I picked it up and took my first puff—just to see what it was all about. I got a little bit in my lungs, coughed, and got dizzy.

But it felt good. After that, I watched passing cars. If someone tossed out a butt, I grabbed it. I scavenged the tobacco scraps left at my house and wandered, head down, in and out of stores and hotel lobbies to rescue butts from ashtrays. I only tried chewing tobacco once, though—in class. The teacher thought it was gum and told me to spit it out. I swallowed it instead. I got sick as a dog.

When I was in the third grade, the principal decided he'd had enough of my bad habits. He put me over his knee and whacked me with a big strap he kept hanging on his office wall. Later that night, my parents saw the purple bruises and asked what had happened. "The principal beat me," I moaned.

"What for?" my mother said, comforting me.

"He caught me smoking."

Their sympathy stopped cold. I don't know what I'd expected, but my father put me over *his* knee and whacked me, too. I didn't cry. I didn't stop smoking, either.

When I was a little older, my uncle Louis sometimes sent me to the store with a note: "Please sell my nephew a pack of Chesterfields." He gave me the money, I showed the note, and the clerk gave me the cigarettes. Of course, I wanted my own cigarettes instead of picking them out of ashtrays and off the street. It's not tough to figure out what I did: I copied my uncle's handwriting for my own note.

But the second time I tried it, I got caught. The store owner had saved one of my uncle's notes and compared the handwriting. He called my mother. I got punished. But I figured out a way to get even with the rat.

The buildings on both sides of his store, and across the street, were industrial. During the summer the heat could be so thick that many establishments didn't close and lock their doors; they just drew a big steel gate across the front and secured that, allowing the air to circulate thoroughly. One Sunday, when no one was at work, I took my fishing pole to the candy store and got a buddy to keep a watch-out. Sure enough, the gate was down but the front door was wide open. The candy and cigarettes display was about eight feet inside the threshold, and I went "fishing" for goodies while my buddy kept his eyes peeled for pedestrians and cars. I did this every Sunday until my mother got suspicious, found my stash, and called the store owner—who called the police.

The police knew and liked my parents, and cut me a lot more slack than I deserved. I took advantage of their good intentions by continuing to misbehave. This time I endured yet another lecture from the police and my parents, and that was that.

———

When I became an altar boy I figured out where the priest kept the wine, and added drinking to my list of bad habits. I also became the leader of my little gang of pals. They called me "the Brain" because I could always come up with ideas about how to get away with something. We stole booze from home-brew beer bootleggers who were just our neighbors. During Prohibition and the Great Depression, they'd make a batch, sell most of it to make ends meet, and drink the rest. You could smell the stuff as you walked down the street. That's how the police found it, too. Our neighbors the Winklers kept a big crock of beer behind a curtain under their kitchen sink. On Saturday nights, when everybody went to the movies, we broke into the house and helped ourselves.

Sometimes we took our plunder to the beach, but after we got caught drinking at Hermosa, I had another idea. By then I was maybe 13. I had a part-time summer job at the local dairy. I helped myself to an empty quart milk bottle, put some white paint in it, and rolled it around so the whole bottle was coated from the inside. I turned it upside down on a newspaper, left it overnight, and the next day, I put it on the garage roof to dry in the sun. The next time we went to the beach we filled that bottle with whatever alcohol we'd stolen, and lay on the sand with only our heads swimming. The lifeguards thought we were clean-cut kids drinking wholesome milk

If we *had* been drinking milk it would have gone well with the pies we stole from Meinzer's Pie Shop. Again, I had masterminded the plot to get revenge. Since businesses were closed on Sundays, markets and restaurants would sometimes give away unused or damaged food to the hungry and needy that came to their back doors near closing time on Saturday night.

By the time we showed up at our local market they had nothing left, so we went to Meinzer's to ask the owner if he had any broken pies they were going to throw out. He was nasty and slammed the screen door.

I was madder than an angry hornet.

I modified my fishing-for-candy-and-cigarettes technique by using a heavy wire and fashioning a hook at the end. I slid the wire carefully through the pie shop's screen and opened the door catch. We grabbed a few pies and ate them at our hideout up on Tree Row. Everyone liked apple, but I've always had a fondness for cherry.

We were so successful that another gang of kids tried the same thing—and got caught. Then they bragged and took credit for our mischief. The arrest made the Torrance paper's front page: MEINZER'S PIE SHOP THIEVES CAUGHT. We waited two days, and then took some more pies, just to show that the police hadn't caught the real culprits. The newspaper ran another story, only smaller: "Meinzer's Pie Shop Robbed Again."

My family must have despaired that I might never turn things around.

———

MY PARENTS, WHO were Catholic, didn't go to church. And when the priest came to the door asking for money, if they didn't have any to give they acted like they weren't home.

I went to church sometimes and once I was late because I'd been goofing off. When I got there the place was jammed. I found an end seat in the back. The priest walked over, grabbed me by the ear, and twisted it. He said, "You go home and get a note from your mother about why you're late."

Boy, I got so mad, I wanted to strike him. Instead, I walked out.

I told my mother, "I'm never going back." Instead, I went with a buddy to his Baptist church, which had a big bell tower. One day, just for fun, I found a huge spool of wire and took some. I climbed into the tower, tied the wire to the bell, and then dropped the rest to the street, where I hoisted it into a nearby pepper tree. After dark I pulled the wire with all my might. Ding-dong! Ding-dong! Lights went on in all the houses. People rushed onto the sidewalks. A woman shouted, "Oh, mama mia, it's a miracle!"

The fire truck came, and the police. I slid out of the tree and disappeared.

I had lots of mischief to spare.

I shot a bull in the scrotum with my BB gun, as well as a dog that bit me while I delivered newspapers. I liberally peppered girls in school with spit wads—and often ended up in a classroom corner for my trouble. Once, when I was wrongly punished for spit wads I hadn't, well—spit—I got back at the teacher by letting the air out of her car tires after school.

I could go on.

Compared to what passes for teens getting into trouble today, I suppose most of what I did seems like kids' stuff. But then the errors of my ways got more serious.

I'd stolen some pies from a bakery truck and the boy who drove it squealed to the police. I had to pay for what I'd taken. But I wanted revenge. I lay in wait and confronted him as he and a friend left the Torrance Theater. We faced off in the alley. At first, a mutual friend of ours volunteered to stand in for me because the driver weighed thirty pounds more than I did, but I knew my friend would just pussyfoot around and no one would get hurt. I had an axe to grind.

"No, that's okay," I said, then suddenly lit into the driver. After many punches, the fight ended when I knocked him down and he rolled into a ditch and lay there bleeding. I went home covered with blood. My mother thought I had been injured. She screamed and my dad came running in. I mumbled some excuse and they left me alone.

When you fistfight, you never think about the real damage you might cause, or somebody dying. When I got up the next morning it bothered me how badly I'd beat up the driver. So much blood. I couldn't stop worrying about what I might have done. I forced myself to go back to where we'd fought. I hoped he wasn't still lying there. Of course, he wasn't, but two days later I saw him in the truck again, his face massively swollen. I was relieved. He was alive. My concern disappeared only to be replaced by excitement: I'd really whooped him.

———

Torrance Police Chief Collier could only tolerate so much. He decided that he had to do *something*, and took me to the local jail to meet some of the inmates. We stopped in front of one cell and stood there for a couple of minutes. The chief said, "Louie. Where do you go on Saturdays?"

"I go to the beach," I said.

"When you're in there," he said, nodding toward the two men in the cell, "you can't go to the beach."

A message started to sink in, but not the message Chief Collier wanted to send. Instead, I realized that I'd have to be smarter about my mischief and not get caught. A couple of days later I stepped out from behind a tree and tossed a handful of tomatoes into a policeman's face. I took off running and was gone by the time his vision cleared.

I wasn't done yet. I discovered that the key to my home also, miraculously, opened the back door to the school gym— allowing my friends and me to get into the basketball games without paying the dime fee. But someone snitched and the locks were changed—and I got taken in again.

This time, everyone who had been willing to put up with me for years had had it. My parents and Pete were tired of the cops coming to the house. The chief of police and the school principal didn't know what to do with me. And to tell you the truth, I didn't much care—except for one thing: I didn't want to be labeled a mental case. Those were different times, and seriously incorrigible kids could be institutionalized and possibly sterilized to prevent those undesirable traits from being passed on to future generations. A common question then, no longer asked, was, "Is there insanity in the family."

Fortunately, we have come a long way.

But then, I thought, perhaps it *was* time for me to change. Could I turn my life around?

———

MY BROTHER, PETE, was always on my side. He tried his best to be a good influence on me. But he was such a good kid that I couldn't compete with him—though I'm not sure why I thought I had to. I guess it was because compared to Pete I knew I was far from good. Pete was never mischievous. He was always a perfect son and a perfect brother. Some kids would hate a "perfect" sibling, but I loved him no matter what.

Besides, when *I* tried to be good, it backfired, like the time my mother and dad went to San Pedro. While they were gone, I scrubbed the kitchen floor. When my parents got back, they said, "Look at the floor! Pete scrubbed the kitchen floor!"

I didn't say a word. Pete said, "It wasn't me. It was Louie." But I still let my folks' first reaction eat at me.

While my parents and the school and the police were trying to decide what to do with me, Pete took me to the local steel mill. The workers looked hot, greasy, and dirty. I said, "My God, what a horrible job." I didn't want to end up like that.

"Yeah? That's what you're going to be doing: just what they're doing, because you haven't put your nose to the grindstone," Pete said.

That vision of my possible future, and the fear of being labeled a hopeless case, finally shocked me into considering that maybe, just maybe I'd taken the wrong path.

Everyone decided to give me one more chance.

I had to participate in school sports.

I was too small for football, so the principal entered me in an interclass track meet, to run the 660-yard race. If I ran, my pile of school demerits would be wiped clean. "If he gets a break," Pete said, "Louie may find that there are other ways of getting attention and being recognized."

The prospect of starting ninth grade with a clean slate was irresistible. All I had to do was run. "I guess I will if you force me to," I told Pete.

"No one is going to force you to do anything," he said, "You're old enough now to make a decision. You can continue in your rotten life and end up in prison or work in a steel mill or an oil field for peanuts. Or you can run and try to accomplish something."

All I had to do was run. No one expected me to win. I didn't disappoint in my first race. I came in last, exhausted, in pain, suffering from being a smoker. I swore to myself I'd never run again. But a week later I had to. It was just as painful except that while coming down the homestretch I heard my classmates cheering for me as I passed another runner. "Come on, Louie!" I didn't realize anyone knew my name. "Come on, Louie!" That time I came in third.

Afterward I realized I had to make a big decision: be a troublemaker or a runner? I loved the new recognition from running, but was it worth it? Yes. I began to train as diligently as I had caused mischief.

It took a few more meets, but I eventually won—and kept winning. No one was more surprised than I was, and by then I was obsessed. I made the All-City Finals in the 660 and placed fifth. Not bad for a kid who would rather have been doing anything else—but needed to save his skin.

Thanks to Pete, who helped guide me in a positive direction, and my own developing positive ambition, I turned my life around. Pete helped out by training with me, which meant he ran behind me and swatted my butt with a switch to keep me moving.

In 1934, while still a high school sophomore, I set a world interscholastic record of 3:17 in the 1320-yard race. Afterward, Pete said he knew I could be a miler—which was just one more lap around the track. "But if you want to be the greatest in the mile you got to run everywhere," he explained. "If the school track is muddy, run around the block"—which I did, in my street clothes. "And never miss a workout. If there's a dust storm, cover your mouth with a handkerchief and get out there and run. If it rains, run." At least it didn't snow in Torrance.

When school got out for the summer I ran anywhere and everywhere. I just ran, ran, and ran. Instead of hitchhiking to the beach, I ran the four miles from Torrance to Redondo. Then I ran two miles along the beach and four miles back to Torrance. I even ran to the store for my mother. I loved the mountains, so I'd head there in my old 1926 Dodge and run around Crystal Lake, jumping over streams and fallen trees and maybe a rattlesnake or two. I'd chase deer down the hill.

I ran all summer long and, without really thinking about it, built an amazing foundation of physical stamina that would later surprise everyone when I competed and kept winning.

But I'll share a little secret: Running around a track never made much sense to me because I kept ending up in the same place I'd started. I felt much better when I was running free, which is just another way of saying that after all the trouble I'd caused as a child, I felt much better just *being* free.

I don't believe anyone is going to argue with me about that.

# The Difference Between Attention and Recognition Is Self-Esteem

I've had many years to wonder why I caused so much mischief and I've come to the conclusion that what I really wanted was recognition. That's not the same as wanting attention. Attention comes and goes, usually quickly. Recognition lasts longer. I wanted to be accepted by the good kids, admired for something. At first my running just got me noticed; with repeated improvement and a go-all-out attitude, notice became recognition. I'd begun to break the negative cycle by taking the first steps to building positive self-esteem through hard work and accomplishments.

But my lack of self-esteem went deep, even when I'd started down a worthwhile path. When I broke the world's high school mile record, there was a party that night. I couldn't face going in alone. I had to wait until somebody else came, and I went in with them. Also, because now everyone knew me, even admired me, I got elected student-body president. But it's not as if I campaigned. And once elected I could barely get up and talk to the kids. Facing a crowd was not like running, which I did alone. I stood behind the auditorium, hoping the teachers would take over, but one of them caught me and took me in. At home, I didn't even tell my mother that I'd won student office. When she found out and asked why I hadn't told her, I just said, "I didn't think it was important."

There are two kinds of self-esteem. I once read in the paper that some people with the highest self-esteem are in prison. Why? Because, for at least a while, they got away with crime, and couldn't imagine that they wouldn't. I had high self-esteem in regards to stealing. Every time I robbed the pie shop and didn't get caught, I became more and more confident and thought the world of myself. But when it came to school and my classmates, I was on shaky ground. My self-esteem was affected by my anxiety over what others thought of me. That weakened my natural confidence. And made me angry. Positive self-esteem must be preceded by self-respect. To get self-respect you have to do something good. Causing mischief wasn't good.

Running was—and it was the first positive thing I did for myself, however reluctantly. My schoolmates' enthusiastic reaction inspired me.

The more I raced, the more they cheered. Because I knew how hard I had to work to win, I began to develop self-respect, and their in-the-moment attention turned into long-term recognition.

I've never forgotten that my fans and family were an important part of my success. Everyone needs that support—even if at first you don't think you do. Look around. See who's on your side and in your corner.

You don't have to go it alone.

# It's Not How You Win,
# It's How You Lose

———

I was just out of high school when my brother called to tell me that he'd entered me to run the 5000-meter race in the first Compton Invitational track meet, held at the Los Angeles Memorial Coliseum in 1936. He knew I had my heart set on trying to make that year's Olympic team as a miler, but Pete said that there were already five great milers in the country. "Wait for the 1940 Tokyo Games to try the mile," he said. "By then you'll be ready." In the meantime, he wanted to see how I'd do against Norman Bright, who, Pete said, would "almost certainly make the Olympic team in this race."

Five thousand meters is twelve and a half laps around the standard 400-meter track. By the last two laps, Bright and I were trading the lead. I thought I could win. But an official made a mistake with a runner that I'd lapped: He motioned him off the track in the wrong direction. Instead of taking a step to the left, he moved across the track to the right. We collided and I tumbled down. I got back up and with a furious kick, angled for the inside. I caught Bright at the finish line, but the excited officials dropped the tape, then they picked it up. Still, I thought it was a dead heat but the officials said that Bright beat me by an inch or two. That's just the way it went.

I always knew that eventually I'd lose a race. After my very first win, I'd gone undefeated for three and a half years, but it was inevitable that one day I would not cross the finish line first. I often wondered how I'd act when that happened. Would I be ashamed? Resentful? Angry? I honestly had no idea.

When I won races they were often by ten, twenty, thirty yards. I'd be on cloud nine. My friends would be all over me with congratulations. My parents would cheer, my girlfriend would hug me. I'd maybe do a radio interview, and watch as friends and family of the other runners consoled them. I could easily picture how the person who beat me would be treated—and wondered if I'd need the consolation I'd seen them get.

When the time came, I was determined to do it right. I wanted to lose cheerfully, so I congratulated Bright honestly. I put my arm around him and said, "That was a brilliant race, and you deserved to win." I had a smile on my face. His mother and father stood there with their mouths open. Then his mother hugged me. That's the way it should be. If you give everything and you lose, so what? It's not going to put you in your grave. I walked away knowing I could handle defeat gracefully, and I had more self-esteem from that than from winning the race.

Today's athletes have far more muscle and better physical fitness programs, faster tracks, and lighter shoes. But some still can't win or lose cheerfully. Perhaps it's because the media puts so much pressure on athletic competition; maybe it's also the potential money for medalists. I wouldn't find it unusual for someone to win a gold medal, imagine all the lucrative endorsement deals to come, and be thinking, "I'm a millionaire!" In my day, we competed for the love of the sport. Performance-enhancing drugs could be had, but no one wanted to win unfairly or damage their health. In my day, we patted the guy who beat us on the back, wished him well, and that was that.

Today it tears me apart when I see an athlete lose and, maybe he or she doesn't cry, but they sit there with their heads down feeling horrible, and sometimes angry with themselves, for everyone to see. It's terrible.

I lost that race to Norman Bright, but I won the next and the next and the next. I was always in the spotlight. And my recognition or fame, for what it's worth, was always with me whether I won or lost. Once you're on top, you're on top. Your achievements are real. They can't take that away from you.

That race began my journey toward securing a berth

on the Olympic team and running the 5000-meter race in Berlin—which wouldn't have happened if I hadn't trusted my brother, Pete, to have my best interests at heart.

Sometimes things look up, sometimes down, but in the end all things work together for good.

By the way, I didn't win the 5000-meter race at the Olympics, but making the team and not winning is like going to the moon and stumbling over a rock and falling. So what? You're still on the moon.

# A Race Isn't Over Until It's Over

After I started at USC on an athletic scholarship, I ran the mile until I went skiing and tore my knee and ankle ligaments and was laid up for three months. But right at the end of track season, because I'd been an Olympian, I was invited to the big Princeton Invitational as a freshman—to run the two-mile race. I won my first national title.

What I really wanted to win was a mile race.

Two years earlier, Pete had taken me to the 1934 NCAA Track and Field national championships in the Los Angeles Coliseum to watch Glenn Cunningham race against Bill Bonthron in the mile. Cunningham had already run an indoor mile at 4:08:04, and had an outdoor time of 4:09.8. I was still, on average, eight seconds behind him. Eight seconds might not seem like much in most situations, but in a mile race it's a lot longer than anyone realizes—about seventy-five yards.

Glenn Cunningham was my hero. I'd read the story of

how he'd been severely burned as a child in a fire that killed his older brother. Much of the flesh on his knees and shins was gone. When bandages were changed, pieces of muscle came out. He also lost all the toes on his left foot. Years later, I saw him in the shower and confirmed what I'd read and heard. He was burned on both legs, up to the middle of his back. The doctors thought his chances of walking again were remote. But Cunningham was not about to give up.

Cunningham epitomized resilience and resolve. He massaged his legs and stimulated blood flow. He endured physical therapy and willed himself to stand and then walk. Soon he began to run. I don't know how he did it, but he was my inspiration. His perseverance made me realize that if I was willing to make the effort and sacrifices, I could be a champion, too. What a great example for any athlete. Cunningham was the greatest ever. I still don't know any story as compelling as his.

He was also a decent man. I once raced against him at an indoor meet. I came up behind him and although I was in better shape, I wouldn't pass him. Out of respect. "Louie, you damn fool," he said. "Run!" So, reluctantly, I did.

We hadn't yet met back in 1934 when I saw him race at the Los Angeles Coliseum and lose to Bill Bonthron, whose time was 4:08.9. I wished the outcome had been different. Then and there I promised myself that someday I'd get that record back for Glenn.

———

IN 1938, I went to Minneapolis with the USC team for the NCAA championships. I was the miler and I felt great, a tiger brimming with adrenaline. The night before the race, Coach Nicholson of Notre Dame came to my room. "I'm ashamed to say this," he said, "but I just came from an East Coast coaches meeting and they're going to tell their milers to do anything they can to knock you out of the race tomorrow. They're going to box you in the last half mile." The eastern coaches were tired of USC's Dean Cromwell being called the world's greatest track coach because USC had won so often—especially when he also had a championship miler. Me.

I was in part responsible because I'd made the mistake of bragging: I'd told someone I was going to go for a four-flat mile because I had been picked by athletes and sportswriters as someone who might be the first to do it.

"I can take care of myself," I told Coach Nicholson. I should have been more appreciative and paid better attention. But you know how kids are: know-it-alls.

The next day on the track, the runners were introduced. Chuck Fenske of Wisconsin had won the mile the year before in 4:13.9. But I had my race planned. I wanted to run the first two laps in 1:58, and then move out, and then sprint the entire last lap to finish with my usual big kick. No one had ever caught me from behind.

Hubris goes before a fall. As Coach Nicholson predicted, the other runners boxed me in—but they didn't wait for the last two laps. I'd say something to the runner next to me, and he'd curse back. One ran his spike through my little toe. Another let his foot trail for a second and, because I was directly behind him, he gashed my right and left shins. Every runner knows that when you're training and a stray dog chases you around the track, all you've got to do is reach back six inches with one foot and catch them in the nose with your spike, and then they won't bother you anymore. A third elbowed me in the ribs and cracked one when I tried to pass him.

I was severely limited until the last 120 yards, when it looked like Fenske, the leader, was far enough ahead. The other runners loosened up. I took advantage and squeezed through and, ignoring my pain, turned it on. I passed Fenske and made for the finish line. I won by five yards.

Coach Cromwell rushed over. "How fast do you think you ran?" he asked. "If I'm lucky I broke 4:20," I said. After all the pushing, shoving, elbowing, and spiking, I thought there was no way I'd run a good race. In fact, when it was clear that I would win, I had slowed down just a bit before the end because I was so disappointed. "Then you're lucky," he said with a grin. "You just broke the national collegiate record. You ran 4:08.03." I couldn't believe it. The record had been Bonthron's 4:08:9.

Mine stood for the next fifteen years.

The next day, a picture of me in the papers showed the extent of how I'd been butchered. I was wrapped in tape and looked like I'd gotten into a hockey brawl. This made victory all the more sweet. I'd won for myself and, as I'd once vowed, for Glenn Cunningham.

(Coincidentally, years later when I met my wife-to-be, Cynthia, she remembered seeing that picture as a child.)

I didn't know it then, but my persistence, perseverance, and unwillingness to accept defeat when things looked all but hopeless were part of the very character traits I would need to make it through World War II alive.

Of course, you don't have to live through a war to have those qualities work for you every day. Sometimes a day in the office or raising the kids is just as challenging.

# Be Prepared

*Louis, at eighty-one, making it look easy, 1998*

# Preparation Determines
# Your Survival

———

Life on earth is dangerous: You should be prepared for anything.

As adults we sometimes encounter circumstances with potentially grave consequences that we can't anticipate. It can seem overwhelming. But each circumstance can usually be broken into smaller, more manageable challenges that we might already be prepared to deal with.

For example, I was in a plane crash at sea during the war. I couldn't do anything about that. I could have died. Instead, I lived. Now what? Rather than try to take on the whole predicament at once, I broke it down to smaller tasks that used the various survival skills I'd already learned: first aid, obtaining food, knowing not to drink salt water, maintaining a positive attitude, and keeping my mind active. I followed my training, a step at a time. I didn't freak out.

You may feel, in your busy life, that learning survival

skills will require too much time that you don't have. Maybe you figure you'll never need them. But you only have one life. You should never be too busy to save it.

Education is the mainstay of being prepared. Every high school should have a survival course. Just one class is all you need. A good hour. You won't learn everything, but you'll know more than when you began—and perhaps create a thirst for more knowledge. A semester course is better. And you could take optional courses to broaden or specialize your knowledge.

I love the outdoors. I've spent lots of time sleeping under the stars, or in a tent: whether in my parents' backyard in Torrance, or camping on the beach, or in the mountains. Growing up, my favorite stories were about Robinson Crusoe and the Swiss Family Robinson. I became an Eagle Scout, and of course the Scout motto is *be prepared*. I learned how to build game traps and catch food. I took classes when possible and tried to learn as much as I could about being prepared for all circumstances.

That came in handy on the life raft.

I love rock climbing. I took courses and practiced when I could. But I've met so-called trained climbers who almost kill themselves through lack of basic knowledge.

I was teaching some kids how to use rock climbing equipment when we heard a guy screaming bloody murder. "What's wrong?" I yelled.

"My girlfriend fell over a cliff," he said, running over.

I followed him to the accident site. She was okay. She'd only slid down the hill to a ledge but had no way to get back up. I secured my rope around a tree and rappelled down and rescued her.

After they got through thanking me, I said, "You're welcome, but what in the world are you doing on this rock? It's shale."

"Oh, we're members of the mountaineer club at Fresno State."

I was annoyed. They'd put me in danger as well as themselves. I suggested that they either give up climbing completely or take some more courses. "The first thing they should teach is what kind of rocks to climb on. This is shale, the most dangerous rock in the world. It separates and slides. You should climb where the rock is hard and you can get hold of it."

At least they hadn't killed themselves. I remember reading about a woman who got into trouble during a day hike on Mount Baldy in Southern California. She had described herself as an experienced climber. She disappeared, and they found her dead three days later. She'd gotten lost, and it got worse from there.

Anything can happen to anyone, but there are simple rules designed to keep you out of trouble. When you're hiking off-trail through the wilderness and you make a turn, break a tree branch so you know that's where you were. Or you can create a pattern of rocks on the ground. When I took groups of camp kids out, I always had a pocketful of ribbons about ten inches long. When we turned I'd tie one to a tree. Then to teach them how not to lose their way, I'd take them up a hill, around it, down, and around again—just to confuse them.

Then I'd say: "I think we're lost."

The response was usually, "Well, we're still following you."

"Yeah, but I'm not sure," I'd say. (Of course, I knew exactly where we were.)

"What are we going to do?"

"What did I teach you?"

They'd been trained, and now they had to use their knowledge.

"Look at the position of the sun," one boy said.

"See which way the stream runs."

"Look for the ribbons," said another.

We set off and each time they found a ribbon I could see their faces shine with the joy of accomplishment. Soon we were back to where we'd started, safe and sound, with the personal reward of having learned a lesson and used it successfully in the real world. It's a great feeling.

Survival, in any situation, from the outdoors to the office, depends on education, preparation, and anticipation.

You've got to think ahead.

# My Survival Kit

Say there's an earthquake or some other natural disaster. It's good to always have a hardhat and a pair of heavy shoes.

"Who has those?" I'll ask when I speak at schools and camps. A few hands might eagerly shoot up. I'll pick someone.

"Where do you keep them?"

"They're somewhere in the house."

"Too late, you're dead. You've got to keep them right near your bed, and once a week just make note again of where they are. You should also put them on every couple of weeks to make sure they're in good condition."

I'll say this again: You only have one life. You should never be too busy to save it.

I spoke at a mountaineering club and afterward some-one asked me a question. "I just read that two guys died on Mount Hood at ten thousand feet even though they built a snow cave to get out of the wind. What happened?"

"They lost their body heat and didn't make it out," I said.

"But maybe if they'd had two items you can put in your shirt pocket, they might have lived."

No one looked like they believed me. "What are they?"

One is a Disney water cape. When you take a water ride they give you one free. (This is probably true at any amusement park.) I buy them by the box. Ten cents apiece, but they're big and will cover your whole body. The other is a shower cap available in any hotel bathroom. Even if you're out of the wind, you're still losing heat through porous clothes and your porous hat. So you put the shower cap over your hat. And you open the cape, cut a slit in the middle, and stick your head through. That'll keep more heat in.

And you can put them both in your shirt pocket.

Besides the water cape and shower cap, I keep a few things in my car at all times. A surgical mask, surgical gloves, leather gloves—to keep from cutting my hands—a rockhound hammer (a geologist's tool used to dig up minerals), a tow rope, jumper cables, a tool kit, a water bottle, and toilet paper.

Anything to help improve my chances.

When I was on the raft, the tool kit included a rubber patch kit, water dye, a flare gun, little air pumps, a mirror made of chromed brass, and a pair of pliers with a screwdriver handle.

But no net to catch fish—on a raft! And worse, where was the knife?

How often I thought: My kingdom for a knife!

Someone hadn't been thinking. You always have to think ahead. Always.

———

BEING STUCK ON a raft in the middle of the Pacific is a pretty exotic circumstance, so let me bring the lesson closer to home. I remember teaching my son, Luke, to drive. He's said that it was more like a course in anticipating what every other driver might do. He was right. I also made him learn how to go in reverse before I'd let him put the car in drive. What on earth for? If you can master keeping the car on a straight line going backward, going forward is much easier.

# Trust What You Know

—————

When you're stuck on a life raft in the middle of the ocean, you're always hungry.

So are the sharks. They were our constant companions, every day circling our makeshift home. At first they were waiting for the tiny bits of bait—small fish we found in the stomachs of the occasional albatross we caught when one landed on the raft (or the bits of albatross we didn't eat)—that I hung overboard on hooks tied to lines wrapped around my fingers, trying to catch a fish. They'd swoop up and take the bait, and the hook. I'd try again and they'd do the same. Sometimes I managed to catch a fish without their interference, but it was rare. The sharks were as hungry as we were. When we said our prayers to be saved, we included a plea not to become a shark's snack.

One night when the guys were asleep a small shark swam by and I decided to put my hand on its head and drag it over the dorsal fin. Why? Who knows? Bored, I guess. I did that twice. They slipped by slowly, and then disappeared—which was unusual.

Suddenly one shot up like a torpedo, with his open mouth right in my face. I automatically hit his snout, shoved him back in the water. Then the other shark came up and I whacked him with an aluminum oar. Mac woke up and reached for the other oar and we beat them back until they'd had enough.

It seemed to me that if they wanted to eat us then turning the tables on them was fair play. The two sharks that had tried to jump into the raft were still with us. Phil and I made a plan. He'd hold the bait, dipping it in and out of the water to get the shark's attention. When it came close I'd grab it by the tail and haul it into the raft—and kill it. When the bait tempted a small one, I leaned over the raft and clutched the tail. Big mistake. Shark skin is gritty like sandpaper and I couldn't hold on because a five-foot shark is stronger than a six-foot man. It quickly pulled me into the ocean. Now it was my turn to shoot out of the water and into the raft.

Here's what happened next, as I described it in *Devil at My Heels*.

*A couple days later we saw some three and four footers, and no larger ones. We hung the bait again. This time I decided to get lower in the raft (to help my center of gravity). I grabbed a passing tail and, as quickly as I could, pulled the shark out of the water. His mouth opened, but Phil was ready, holding an empty flare cartridge. He shoved it in. The shark instinctively closed his mouth and wouldn't let go of the cartridge. I took the screwdriver end of the pliers from our emergency kit, rammed it through his eye, into his brain, and killed him.*

*Ripping a shark open without a knife is a very tough job. I'd used the pliers to fashion saw-like teeth on one corner of our chromed-brass mirror. Though sharp enough to open a man's arm like butter, the shark skin put up a fight. It took almost ten minutes to cut through the belly.*

*Because of a survival course I'd taken on base in Hawaii about how to deal with sharks, I knew that eating raw shark meat would make us sick. The smell, a bit like ammonia, was bad enough. The only edible part was the liver.*

I knew that shark liver was a rich source of vitamins and protein. The minute we ate it we got a big boost. We had a luscious, gooey, bloody meal of shark liver twice and it was the best thing that happened to us.

Imagine then my surprise when years later a television show criticized me for eating sharks' liver, and quoted someone from the military saying, "That's where all the poison goes." What poison? Just as when a human eats, a shark's liver takes care of anything unsatisfactory. Then you pee it out or otherwise. There aren't any toxins left in the liver, especially that of a wild shark.

Here's further proof: I heard that during a break in shooting *Unbroken* in Australia, the actors playing me, Phil, and Mac ate raw shark liver. No one got ill.

If I hadn't trusted what I knew, who knows if I'd be here to tell this story. Those mouthfuls of shark liver might have made all the difference.

# Keep Your Mind Sharp

Every day we put our brains through their paces, but the older we get the more it's necessary. You have to stay active. Engage with others. Don't sit and vegetate in front of the television. Move your body. Use your head.

You've heard that kind of advice before, but I proved it to myself when I was adrift on the Pacific Ocean. I'd taken physiology classes at USC with Dr. Roberts. He'd said, "The brain is a muscle. It's essential to exercise it or it will atrophy." I believed him. Despite hunger, thirst, heat, desperation, weight loss, boredom, and ravenous sharks, I worked my brain whenever I could. I hate mathematics, but I'd lie there and add up a column of figures in my head. Then I'd try a double column. I may not have gotten the right answers, but I wasn't letting my brain go to sleep.

To deal with hunger, the pilot, Russell Philips, and I described in intricate detail meals we'd cooked or eaten, right down to the smallest ingredients, and then how it tasted.

That was an exhaustive, extensive exercise. I had to be very precise: how much salt, how much baking powder, how long to knead the dough, how to make the finished product crispier, how long to bake at what temperature, how to make spaghetti sauce, how to stuff a turkey, how to make stuffing, how long to bake the turkey, how crisp the skin should be. The guys got so hungry they were on me to do this every day, so I became the main cook. I didn't mind, and flung myself into making meals by the seat of my pants. My mother was the same way. We even washed our imaginary dishes, dried and put them away. Anything to use our brains. This routine may sound frivolous, but it was great because it kept us focused on something positive, rather than letting the desperate reality of our situation overwhelm us.

We also shared stories from our pasts. We sang. Phil and I talked about contraptions we wanted to invent. We talked about the future, our plans.

"What are you going to do after the war?" Phil asked me.

"I want to convert the PE depot [a railroad freight depot] in my hometown into a nice restaurant with a bar." Then I'd describe what it would look like inside, and all the rest, right down to the tiniest detail.

———

WHILE STUCK ON the raft, the lack of the usual input we have in our lives must have cleared some space in my head because

I started to remember things that I shouldn't have been able to recall—events that happened to me when I was two and three. For instance, although I was born in Olean, New York, my parents moved to Southern California when I was two. We could only afford to travel by rail. At Grand Central, my mother walked Pete and me along the platform and into the train. But a couple of minutes after rolling out, she couldn't find me anywhere. She searched all the cars and then did it again. Frantic, she demanded the conductor back up to New York—and she wouldn't take no for an answer. That's where they found me: waiting on the platform, saying, "I knew you'd come back," in Italian. When I got home from the war, I told my mother, and she was amazed that I remembered.

When Phil and I were "rescued" by the Japanese, we were just as sharp as the day we crashed—only many pounds lighter. I thought to myself, "Six weeks ago, I was a world-class athlete." And then, for the first time in my life, I cried.

The enemy sailors took us aboard and tied us to the mast. They hit Phil with a pistol across the face. But as they went to strike at me, I knew enough to throw my head back and hit the mast instead. For what it's worth, they did it just to save face and prove their superiority. Otherwise they weren't unkind to us, more like surprised we were still alive and coherent.

During our first interrogation on Wotje Atoll, where our captors took us before sending us to Kwajalein—Execution

Island—the interviewers were astounded at our sharpness. They brought officers in to speak with us. If we were a bunch of mushy-headed dummies that had lost our brains to the vast salt water, they wouldn't have bothered. I like to think that my wits helped keep me alive until the war ended. Use it or lose it.

On Kwajalein we were taunted, harassed, spit upon, jabbed with sticks, starved, and medically experimented upon with near-deadly injections. The food we got, if you can call it food, was filthy. We'd eat it and it would go right through us. If we were going to have a mental breakdown, it should have been then. And yet, when the interrogation started, I was sharp enough to deceive our captors.

They liked to manipulate me. I'd be brought into a room where biscuits, pastries, and sodas lay on a table. The Japanese puffed on cigarettes and blew the smoke in my face. I wasn't a heavy smoker, but I wanted one badly. I knew that if I gave them the information they wanted, I'd get a reward.

I wanted the reward but not because I'd betrayed my country. I decided to try and trick them. In Hawaii we'd constructed three mock airfields with phony airplanes, so if the Japanese came they'd bomb the wrong field. I knew one of them was right near Hickam. When they brought up airfields in Hawaii and I went, "Well, uh . . . ," they thought they had me. I pretended to try and avoid the question, but they kept on me and finally I broke down, saying, "Okay, okay. There's one here"—and I gave them the fake field—"one here, one there, and one there."

I got a biscuit and a little soda pop. They were pleased. I had out-thought my captors on Execution Island, been rewarded, and managed to live another day.

Unfortunately, other than Phil and myself, I know of no other prisoners who made it off Kwajalein alive. We were lucky. As we discovered years later, one Japanese officer knew that I was a track star and recommended that Phil and I be spared because we might be better used for propaganda purposes.

# Don't Forget to Laugh

War is serious stuff. Life is, too. Laughter helps us make it through.

When I was based at Hickam Field in Hawaii during World War II, the soldier in charge of the base Officers' Club had to keep the billiard tables and the slot machines in good repair. He also cashed our paychecks. For some reason he was always irritable when we showed up; later we found out that although he was a lieutenant, we made more than he did because of flight pay. He complained every time we went in. "I put up with more stuff than you do," he told me. "You go up there, you enjoy flying, and you get paid extra money for it." Right. I really enjoy flying and getting shot at, I thought.

I said, "Why don't you come up with us and fly the plane, and see how difficult it is."

Of course it's not that difficult—takeoffs and, especially, landings are more dangerous.

He agreed. We put him in the copilot's seat. I had to crawl

through the nose to go down to the navigator's table. Right in front of the navigator's table are the chains that connect to the pilot's foot pedals. They work on something like a motorcycle chain, up and down. We're on the intercom and the pilot says, "Okay, I'm turning it over to . . ."

The minute the lieutenant took the controls, I pulled down on the pedal chain from below. Then I suddenly pulled up on the chain. The plane jerked, and he screamed. I did this a couple of times until he gave up and the pilot took over.

The pilot asked him, "What's wrong? This flies almost by itself."

"Well, give me another try," the lieutenant said.

I pulled the same stunt.

He finally gave up and said, "Well, I guess you guys really do earn your flight pay."

After he was gone, we had a good laugh. Sure, we wanted to put him in his place, but we weren't trying to be mean. We'd lost so many planes. Eleven in one year just around the islands. We could go down in a raid at any time. We had to have a sense of humor and an outlet for the anxiety lest it get the better of us.

One of my best stunts only involved a bit of chewing gum.

At Hickam, we were supposed to take off and follow various headings to test the accuracy of our plane's compass. While the ground crew readied the aircraft, and before any crew showed up, I walked around the ship, casually chewing gum, like I was doing an inspection. My destination was the two small holes near the nose that were the drain openings for hoses in the cockpit that connected to the pilot relief tubes; in other words, funnels into which the pilot and copilot peed while flying. The urine ran down the hoses and the wind sucked it out.

I plugged both holes with gum. It was revenge because some of my private rations had gone missing.

When the crew showed up, I went to my post in the bomb bay and we taxied to the end of the runway for takeoff.

Procedure called for closing the bomb-bay doors just prior to hitting the gas. Before the doors shut I dropped onto the tarmac and dashed off the runway. Russell Philips took off assuming I was on board. Instead, I headed for Honolulu.

Later, the engineer gave me a blow-by-blow description of all the fun I'd missed. When Phil had to pee he used his funnel. Instead of emptying, it filled to the brim. Phil needed one hand to balance the funnel so it didn't spill. He had no idea why there was a problem so he called the engineer, who decided he should pour the excess into the copilot's funnel. The copilot didn't mind, but first he wanted to take his leak. When his funnel filled as well, no one could believe it. Two malfunctions simultaneously?

There they were, balancing their funnels and trying to fly. When they hit some turbulence it was all over.

The engineer found the problem after landing, and pulled

out the gum. By then everyone realized I wasn't aboard. They came looking for me. But I was already gone.

When I got back they were half pissed, half laughing. My punishment was to pay for a few beers, after which they felt much better.

————

We also had to find ways to laugh in POW camp—anything to keep away the dread.

At Camp 4-B, in Naoetsu in northwestern Japan, the place was infested with rats. I slept on the upper deck of a two-tier bunk, and the rats—sometimes as big as rabbits—had no fear. Occasionally I could feel them at night, running over my stomach, stopping, moving on to the next man. If you tried to push them away, they'd bite you.

Enough was enough. I made a crude paddle and slept with it right across my throat. Sure enough, one night a huge rat walked onto my belly and stopped there. I gripped the paddle and went WHACK! Everybody heard that—and the loud, surprised squeak that followed. The whole place broke into laughter. I didn't kill the rat, but I must have stunned him as he was a little slow in scrambling away. We'd scored one for our side and it felt good.

Being overrun by rats is of course no laughing matter, but it was an inescapable truth. The best humor is based on truth when it lets us acknowledge an uncomfortable or unmentionable yet common experience. You feel better if only for a moment.

Besides, given our situation we knew that the rats had it nearly as bad as we did. Maybe they were laughing at the insanity of it all, as well.

# Don't Give Up,
# Don't Give In

★

*The day after liberation from Naoetsu, 1945.
Louis, front row, third from the left.*

# You Are the Content
# of Your Character

———

After drifting almost two thousand miles west on the Pacific Ocean, Phil and I were "rescued" by the Japanese—Mac had died on the thirty-third day and we'd committed his body to the sea—and eventually shuffled from prison camp to prison camp. I spent a year at Ofuna, a secret interrogation facility near Yokohama, and was then transferred to Omori prison camp, located on a man-made island on Tokyo Bay. There I was punished relentlessly even though I'd done nothing wrong.

My troubles started on the first day when Mutsuhiro Watanabe, a brutal prison guard that had been nicknamed the Bird before I got there—if we'd called him something filthy, as he deserved, and he found out, he might have punished the whole camp— singled me out.

We were lined up and he came out strutting, acting like a god. He walked by and looked everybody over, stopping in front of each person. He looked at me. His eyes were black and sadistic. I looked away. Whack! He knocked me down. Apparently, if you looked away he punished you. "Why you no look in my eyes?" This time I did look. The problem was that if you looked he also knocked you down. I was on the ground, bleeding. He pulled out a tissue, as if he were sorry, and reached down and handed it to me. I thought, *Oh, the guy can't be all that bad*. I dabbed the blood coming out of my head and I stood up. Bang, he hit me again. Down I went, and this time I had no illusions that he was a psychopath— and I was completely at his mercy.

Thereafter he always hounded me. I tried to stay in the background, but he'd find me. He'd come to the barracks with two guards and call everyone to attention. He'd look around the room and come straight for me. "You come to attention last," he'd say, then take off his big belt with a big steel buckle, and crack me across the head.

If it wasn't one thing, it was another.

The Bird, a sergeant, couldn't handle power. He had a camp full of high-ranking officers—submarine commanders, colonels, captains, lieutenants—and must have felt like a kid in a candy store. He realized he could tell us what to do, and it kind of went to his head. If we hesitated after he gave us an order we'd get beaten. He didn't really need an excuse, though. I had it rough, but other prisoners sometimes had it worse. The bottom line is that we were all extremely obedient.

When the Bird abused me, I was angry. I have Italian blood. I wouldn't show it, but I had revenge written all over my heart where he couldn't see it. It wasn't the pain, it was the humiliation. Who likes to be humiliated? You feel like a nobody. I'm a survivor and I wouldn't give up, but I hated the Bird even more than I hated sharks. I would never say, "Oh, well, the shark's only hungry." "Oh well, the Bird is just doing his job." No. Anything that's trying to kill you is your enemy.

One day, instead of a beating, the Bird surprised me by asking if I'd consider making a broadcast at Radio Tokyo. I had no intention of participating in anything treasonous or morally suspect. On the other hand, a broadcast might be a way to let my family know that I was still alive. (I didn't know it, but since Omori was a secret camp, no one at home knew what had happened to me. They assumed the worst.) I talked to the senior officers at camp to find out what they thought. I was shocked when they didn't object. Other prisoners had done the same, they explained, using the opportunity to send sly messages back home without compromising themselves. I made a plan.

I told the Bird I would do it. Two men from Radio Tokyo (or so they said; they were probably intelligence officers) asked me to write my own speech.

On November 18, 1944, they drove me to the radio station and gave me the grand tour. Radio Tokyo was in a beautiful new building. I had lunch in their American-style cafeteria. They showed me hotel-style rooms with beds and linens— very different from the plank I slept on at Omori. This was seduction at its most intense.

I made my broadcast, and managed to slip in messages that other soldiers were also alive. I wouldn't know this for many months, but news of my broadcast brought joy to friends and my family. It seems my parents had already received the letter from President Roosevelt declaring me dead. So they were beside themselves at the news that rumors of my demise were premature, to say the least.

———

TWO WEEKS LATER the two "employees" of Radio Tokyo brought me back to the station. They complimented my "beautiful radio voice," gave me a heavy winter overcoat, and took me to the cafeteria. There I met one American and two Australian soldiers who the Japanese said were also doing broadcasts—and enjoying the benefits of cooperation. All three shook my hand but kept their eyes downcast at the floor. To me, that read clearly as, "Hey, I'm sorry I got into this mess. I'm ashamed. Don't do it."

I wish they'd taken their own unspoken advice. But I now knew that the whole rationale behind being singled out almost daily for the Bird's brutal attention was to soften me up to be used as a propaganda pawn. Why? Because I wasn't simply an unknown soldier. I was well-known at a time when winning athletes were like movie stars. (Nothing's changed.) When the miserable are offered a better life, most will accept it. The three soldiers I'd met were willing to exchange cooperation for a clean bed and some food.

Had I been allowed to write my own script again, or speak off the cuff—anything that wouldn't compromise me or smell of treason—I might have taken the opportunity to be on the radio again. But this time the intelligence agents wanted me to read what *they'd* written.

I read a few sentences to myself. It stunk.

I said, "No, I can't read this."

"But you must read it."

"No. First of all, it doesn't sound like me." I shouldn't have said that because they thought they just had to change a few words to make me happy. I declined their offer. "No. I positively cannot read this."

Here's how their script began, exactly as they typed it: *"Well, believe it or not . . . I guess I'm one of those 'lucky guys,' or maybe I'm really unlucky . . . Anyway . . . here's me, Louis Zamperini, age, 27, hometown Los Angeles, California, good ole United States of America speaking. What I mean by lucky is that I'm still alive and healthy . . ."*

They walked out of the room and had a conference. While they were gone I snuck a copy of the speech into my pocket and prayed they wouldn't miss it. When they returned one said, "Because you refuse to read this, I think you go to punishment camp."

*I think?* Did he mean that I had one last chance to reconsider?

"No, I positively can't do it," I insisted. I'd taken an oath as an officer and made a promise as an American to be loyal and defend my country. The Japanese could punish me all they wanted to, but they couldn't change my character. Without it, I was nothing.

I also realized that despite being threatened with punishment camp, saying no to the second broadcast might actually work in my favor. If I had to switch camps, then at least I'd be away from the Bird. Anything would be better than the way I currently lived.

To my surprise, the Bird was transferred before I was—maybe he'd been punished because I wouldn't cooperate. Eventually, my turn came. On March 1, 1945, I was sent by train to Naoetsu, 250 miles northwest of Tokyo.

We lined up in the courtyard of camp 4-B for an inspection. Snow covered the ground in ten- to twelve-foot drifts. The icy minutes dragged by. Finally, the company commander emerged from a tin shack. It was the Bird.

As I wrote in *Devil at My Heels*, "*I steadied myself on the man next to me in line. But inside I gave up all hope. I thought, Oh, what they've done to me! This is futile. There's*

*no escape. It was the lowest ebb. The cruelest joke. The kiss
of death. I realized I'd never get away from the Bird.*

*"Watanabe marched down the line and found me. His
black eyes bored into mine. It was impossible to look at him,
and impossible to look away. His face twisted into a sick,
sardonic smile. He didn't seem at all surprised to see me."*

But I couldn't give up hope. Not my style. I would do what
I had to do to survive. From that moment until the end of the
war, when we were freed, I would really come to understand
the meaning of "Don't give up, don't give in."

# Never Let Anyone Destroy Your Dignity

During the two-plus years I lived in Japanese prisoner-of-war camps, I noticed that the soldiers who suffered the most were the ones who wouldn't accept their situations. We needed all our meager strength and mental energy simply to get through the day. Those guys drained their personal resources by refusing to accept our (we all hoped) temporary lot. I decided to consider my incarceration as a challenge—like winning a race. That gave me purpose. Sure, I wished I was home with my family, but I had to deal with the reality.

I had taken the Bird's daily beatings at Omori, and then at Naoetsu. I had to. I never complained. I just got knocked down, bled, got up, got knocked down, bled, got up. I expected it. I wouldn't let it get me down. Sometimes it took me two days to recover, but I always had a positive attitude. Steely, but positive. No way would he break me.

One day the Bird asked me to take care of a goat and warned, "If the goat dies, you die." The goat died. I knew he could kill me, but he chose instead to humiliate me. Maybe he thought he would finally break me, but I can't really guess what was in his head. My punishment: hold a heavy wooden plank above my head while he watched—and watched, and watched.

I lasted thirty-seven minutes. A camp-mate timed it. Brutal. No one could believe, least of all the Bird, that I didn't give in. I might have gone longer but the Bird punched me in the stomach, causing me to drop the plank.

The great lesson of my life is perseverance. Never give up. It's like my brother said, "Isn't one minute of pain worth a lifetime of glory?"

I wasn't reaching for glory at Naoetsu. I just wouldn't give the Bird the satisfaction of destroying my dignity. Don't let anyone take yours away, either.

# Hate Is a Personal Decision

Long after I'd come back from the war, I spoke at a middle school near my home. A few days later, I got a stack of letters from the students. In one, a girl wrote, "After you left I went to a girl in my class who I've hated for two years and asked her to forgive me. Now we're the best of friends."

Beautiful.

When I counseled troubled kids, I found that they had lots of serious hate: for their situations, sometimes their families, society, the rules, and often themselves. I knew from my own experience that there is a twisted kind of satisfaction that comes from hating. You hate and hate and hate, and think you're getting even by hating. But it's a ruse. It's a cover-up. Hate destroys—but not the object of your hatred. It destroys you.

Hate is more damaging than alcoholism. Alcoholism is a disease.

Hate is a personal decision.

A war buddy lost a leg in Japan, but he survived the conflict and the prison camp. After the Japanese surrender, we traveled home from Manila and stayed together in the hospital in Hawaii. Sometimes we'd go to the beach. He never wanted anyone to think of him as handicapped because he was a one-legged-man, so sometimes, just for the heck of it, we'd wrestle. He was heavier and stronger and people seemed to get a big kick out of watching us having fun.

Back in the States he was fitted with a prosthetic leg, and we'd go out on the town—to the Florentine Gardens and other dinner clubs in Hollywood. He'd have a great time, even dancing. In those days, because we were veterans, we could get dinner, drinks, and almost everything for free if we'd just get up and say a few words during intermission. This happened a lot to me because thanks to the press and the photographers who trailed me, I was something of a celebrity.

It sounds like fun, right? But my friend was falling apart inside, and it gradually became apparent from the outside. He wouldn't eat rice in the prison camp, and he never touched it after the war. He grew increasingly bitter, and his hate became more and more intense. He ended up working in the control tower at LAX, and I used to drop by. It didn't take long before he'd get on to how he hated the Japanese because they'd cut his leg off when it wasn't necessary. Maybe so, but that was the past. He had his whole life ahead of him, but he couldn't embrace the present or the future. His hate had destroyed his spirit.

If you cling to the axe you're grinding, eventually you'll only hurt yourself.

# The True Definition of Hero

I never think of myself as a hero. I can't stop people from saying what they want to say, but I always keep in mind a verse from Proverbs: "Let others boast of you, but not with thine own mouth." (I guess even God thinks it's better to have someone else be your PR man.)

"Hero" is an easy word for people to use and maybe overuse. These days anyone who does anything that involves encountering danger is called a hero. I understand the sentiment, and I support the brave men and women on the front lines as police and firefighters and soldiers. I have nothing but the greatest respect for someone who puts themselves in harm's way for another, and for those who do good deeds above and beyond the call of duty, like being a teacher or a doctor where most fear to tread. I suppose we can't have enough heroes among us, but I don't apply that word to myself. When I speak somewhere, say at a Veterans' Day or Memorial Day observance, and I'm introduced as an "Olympian and a war hero," I correct that. The heroes are the men and women sitting in the audience with missing legs or arms, or a mother or dad who lost their kid in the war, or a brother or sister.

I said the same when I used to speak on cruise ships. I knew there were veterans aboard, and some senior citizens, some of whom had gone to war—didn't matter which one—and I didn't want to make myself any more special than they were.

I wasn't.

Whatever I did in the war, I did for myself and my fellow soldiers. I did not do it because I wanted to be heroic, but because that's what I was trained to do. I did my part without question. I remembered my family rules: You have to work for the betterment of everyone. If I know I can do something, why should someone else risk *their* life?

Once, while talking to an old soldier about the war, he kept knocking his wooden knee. I knocked it—respectfully—and said, "Where'd you leave that?"

"I left it in Palau," he said, referring to an island in the Pacific.

He's a hero. I'm just a survivor.

# Attitude Is Everything

★

*Forgiving former prison guards in Japan, 1950.*

# You Must Have Hope

There's the soldier who says, "Ah, the war's gonna be over in three months." If he keeps saying that, no matter if he's right or wrong—and if he isn't in the wrong place at the same time as a bullet or a bomb—he has a good chance to survive mentally intact.

But the guy who sits back and says, "Yeah, you guys are a bunch of optimists. The war's never going to end," has less of a chance.

I had a friend just like that in prison camp. He'd sit in the yard and stare at the ground. He wouldn't talk to us. When we'd quietly trade gossip we'd heard—"The Normandy invasion is taking place. The war's going to be over before Christmas"—he refused to participate.

After the war, the Army sent me to Florida for my rest cure. That's where I met my future wife, Cynthia Applewhite. One day we were sitting around at the beach club with a bunch of Air Corps guys, discussing how the human mind functions in war—and suddenly I see that very guy from my prison camp come in. He sat by the pool. He stared at the ground. He hardly talked. Nothing had changed. He may have made it home alive, but to me, he didn't make it.

This can happen in any stressful situation. It's not just about the war.

You must have hope. It rejuvenates your whole being. You can't allow negative thinking—even if you know your chances are slim. I'm not saying that it's easy to do, but the ability to envision the road to successful completion is what keeps you alive.

Hope provides the power of the soul to endure.

# Don't Ask Why, Ask What's Next

I've been blessed with a long life of good health as a result of a beneficial lifestyle—a combination of exercise, diet, charity, and cheerfulness. At my age the best exercise is walking. The family got me a wheelchair a year ago. I understand. But I still insisted on walking as much as possible. Around the house. To the car. I *have* to walk because it keeps my blood circulating. Walking keeps my legs powerful. Walking is probably the best type of moderate exercise there is. I've fallen a couple of times, but I can't afford to quit. When I need to I'll use a cane to give me a third point of contact. But I still try to walk around the house as much as I can without the cane. People shouldn't give up walking!

Now, I'm 97 years old. Am I surprised that I'm still here when most of the people I knew are gone—most of my friends, buddies from the war? Sure. But I don't feel guilty. And I'm not lonely. My attitude is to just accept it. It is what it is. Instead of getting all caught up in asking *why*, I ask, *what's next?* That's all you have to know.

Whenever I've had to go to the hospital, and the doctors tell me how long I'll have to stay, I always try to get better sooner. So far, it's worked. Why? I help heal my body by—again—accepting the situation. I let the doctors do what they can, but in the meantime I also use the healing powers of cheerfulness. When I leave early, the doctors always credit my attitude.

If you can't control your attitude, forget it. You're going to heal slowly or die young.

A side benefit of my cheerful attitude is that the nurses fight over me. They're used to having a bunch of guys who grimace and complain. This isn't to say that they don't accept each patient and their particular needs for who they are; sometimes groaning and grimacing is all you can do. But I cause less stress for everyone, including me.

The nurses come in to talk, and end up lingering. I remember one tall and beautiful blond nurse who said, "Oh, Louie, you're a Trojan! I also went to USC." We talked about football. About her. A little bit about me. Finally she got around to the reason for her visit. "I came to give you a shot," she said. "In the buttocks. So roll over." After she accomplished her mission, she said, "I'm sorry, Louie. I've gotta leave you now."

"You've gotta leave me *now*?" I said. "You know that you're the first woman who ever said that to me!"

She came back later and brought six other nurses to meet me. When I left the hospital there were nine nurses waiting to have their pictures taken with me.

Having a positive attitude pays off in ways that you can't even imagine, yet stay forever in your memory.

# *You* Choose How to View Your Fate

Conventional wisdom says that if you're marooned like Tom Hanks was in the movie *Cast Away* you'll go stir-crazy, or batty. I have the opposite opinion. I think that guy had it made! He wasn't in solitary confinement in a tiny concrete cell. He didn't lose his freedom like a prisoner of war. Yes, he missed his family and friends, but wouldn't you rather be free on an island, with fish to catch, fruit to eat, and nice beaches to walk along than to be someone's prisoner? I'd rather be alone there for the rest of my life than spend one minute caged.

Why? It's a beautiful life. Everything you'll have to do to survive is an accomplishment. You figure out how to catch the fish: What an accomplishment! What a thrill. You figure out how to get food: What an accomplishment! You figure out how to build a hut. Great. That's why Boy Scouting was so exciting: Every time I won a merit badge, I had accomplished something.

On a deserted island, a castaway should be the happiest guy in the world. Even if he is—at that moment—the only guy in the world.

Maybe the toughest part of being a castaway is readjusting to society after you're rescued. You no longer get to do everything your way.

I'm not saying being alone on an island is a better life than being in your own home, with your family and friends and familiar things. I'm suggesting that you can choose to view your fate in a more positive fashion. You just have to be willing to try.

# The Secret of Contentment

When the Apostle Paul was imprisoned, he said, "Whatever situation I find myself in, I have learned thereby to be content." In more modern words, it means that while you can't always control what happens in life, you can control your reaction to it.

To be content, you have to accept everything. If you can make that attitude part of who you are then nothing can bother you. It might be tough at first, but soon it becomes a habit.

When my bomber crashed into the Pacific Ocean, I didn't *want* to be stuck on a raft in the middle of nowhere. But there we were. We expected to be rescued shortly, but weren't. Now we had to do everything to survive. I didn't argue with what had happened, or imagine "if only" alternatives. I accepted our situation and let my training take over. I was *in control* of myself because I accepted things; to begrudge them was a waste of time and energy. Acceptance made it easier for me to deal with what I had to do to stay alive moment by moment, day by day. You must work willingly with what you have. Why make it tough on yourself and others by having a bad attitude?

All my life I've been a positive person—even when I was a troublemaker as a kid. It makes sense: I was positive I could get away with whatever mischief I was up to. If I didn't, I was positive I could talk my way out of trouble—and most of the time I did. I lived in the moment and dealt with the rewards or the consequences later. Same on the raft: I took advantage of my situation to learn whatever I needed to learn in order to live another day, to avoid being a shark's afternoon snack.

If you think that no one in my situation could have been cheerful, you're missing the point. *Acceptance creates cheerfulness*, which in turn creates contentment.

———

ANGELINA JOLIE, WHO directed *Unbroken*, has come to visit me many times. I've never met a woman like her. She's a human dynamo. She takes up any challenge that comes along. Her desire is to overcome. She doesn't brag. She gives instead of takes. She has a sweet and charitable heart for the underdog. She's a doll. She loves me and I love her. She brought me chocolate for Valentine's Day, and always a great bottle of wine.

She even lives in my neighborhood. We can wave to each other.

When Angelina got back from filming *Unbroken* in Australia she showed up at my house and said, "Louie, now I love you twice as much." We hugged and held hands.

That was nice to hear. I said, "You're lucky I'm not twenty-one."

Brad was also there. I shrugged my shoulders. I love Brad, but what else could I do?

One time Angelina kissed me on the lips. Man! I know there are millions of men in the world who probably wished they were me at that moment.

Again, what could I do? I had to accept the situation cheerfully.

Like the Apostle Paul says: "Whatever situation I find myself in I learn thereby to be content."

Angelina kissing me? I was content.

Attitude is everything.

This is the secret.

# After the War:
# Still Lost

*The* Flyaway *before the storm, 1948.*

# You Can't Run (or Sail)
# Away from Yourself

LOS ANGELES TIMES, *front-page lead story*

DATELINE: *Monday, March 8, 1948*

   HEADLINE: ZAMPERINI, L.A. WAR HERO,

   MISSING ON BOAT AT SEA

      SUBHEAD: *Craft Last Heard From on Feb. 28*

*Louis Zamperini, former SC track star who survived 47 days
on a life raft in the Pacific during the war, is one of a crew of
10 aboard the 60-foot schooner* Flyaway, *unheard from since
Feb. 28.*

*The U.S. Coast Guard yesterday released a marine broadcast
to all ships asking for information on the* Flyaway *and sent
an inquiry to officials of Acapulco, Mex. for information . . .*

I came home from the war to find myself a celebrity, a war survivor, and well-known athlete who, because I'd been housed

for a time in a secret interrogation camp, had been presumed dead. But even after my family learned I was alive, no one knew if I'd actually make it back. When I did, the true story broke in the *New York Times*, made headlines everywhere, and I was interviewed constantly and in demand as a speaker.

After marrying Cynthia in 1946, we were invited as a couple to many social functions: new theater openings, movie premieres, and sophisticated parties. For instance, we were at the opening of the gangster Bugsy Siegel's Flamingo Casino in Las Vegas. There I met Siegel's girlfriend, or as they say in the movies, his moll: Virginia Hill. She was gracious and gorgeous and we got on like old friends.

The high life was fun but I needed to get established and settle down. Edwin W. Pauley, the oilman (UCLA's Pauley Pavilion is named after him), wanted me to run for the California state legislature. "I want you in Sacramento," he said. I didn't understand why—and the job only paid eighteen hundred dollars for two years. But then I noticed that three guys on the state legislature whom I'd met had beautiful homes and a boat in the harbor. Hey, this is great, I thought.

I started going to various political functions and informal gatherings. One was at a bar in downtown Los Angeles, owned by a guy named Joe. He also owned a bowling alley. We met there at least once a month, sometimes twice a month. The dinner was always venison cacciatore. Joe would pour drinks for us, and one for himself, and say, "First one today!" Probably the hundredth, but he'd always say it was the first. I asked him about the venison, and he said a couple of city officials went into Griffith Park with a .22 rifle and got him all the deer he wanted.

Everybody drank, but I didn't want to get drunk around these folks. I wanted to listen. What I learned was that to the people in charge I would be just a vote. There was talk about passing a law that all the oil rigs—and there were many all over Southern California in those days—had to have fences around them. It would cost millions. My job would be to vote against that, and I'd get paid under the table. I started putting two and two together: That's how these guys were able to afford those nice houses and boats. You couldn't get them by being honest; or at least not as quickly. I probably could have been elected, but then I'd have had to vote the way they wanted. That just didn't seem right, both morally, and personally. I moved on.

———

WHEN YOU GET down to it, your reputation and character are all you have. I valued mine and I had to remain consistent. Otherwise, how would I make money to support my family and the kids we planned to have?

Although I wasn't interested in being a political pawn, I still thought it would be a good idea to get rich as quickly as possible.

My first venture was war surplus. I bid on twenty or thirty Quonset huts and sold them to the movie studios, who wanted all they could get for storage. Next I went into repairing and selling wartime ice boxes. They needed hinges and lids. I fixed and moved a bunch of those.

Then in the beginning of 1948 an irresistible opportunity came along. Two USC buddies, one from El Salvador and the other from Los Angeles, said they had some large D8 Caterpillar tractors in the Philippines and seven thousand dollars would hold them for us; then we could have them shipped to Los Angeles and turn a tidy profit. My buddies had both majored in business in college, so I depended on them. They introduced me to their contact from Hawaii, who said, "No problem. I've got control of everything," just before he left for home to close the deal. He just needed the $7,000 earnest money. I went to the bank and got him a cashier's check. Then we waited. And waited. Occasionally we'd get a letter: "Everything's going great." And waited some more.

The delay was making me crazy. I needed something positive to happen and I couldn't just sit around counting the seconds.

Maybe, I thought, a change of scenery would relieve some of the pressure. I could relax and refocus.

I needed that. I was also suffering from what we now call post-traumatic stress disorder. I drank, fought, and had terrible nightmares about the Bird. It was as if the war were still going on in my head. If I was in horrible shape I couldn't be of use to myself—or anyone else.

I had known for some time that there was trouble in paradise, by which I mean at home. Although Cynthia often went to parties and other functions with me, she grew to dislike the lifestyle. The postwar celebrations went on for a long time and she got fed up with it. She refused to go to from bar to bar, or from party to party, with booze all over the place. Instead she stayed home or went to a movie or spent time with friends. But it was pretty rough on her. We were still in a small starter apartment in East Hollywood, not much more than a room. With everyone back from the war, housing was tough to find.

One night my car got stolen, or so I thought. I got drunk at a place called Nickodell, a restaurant with a big bar. I was there with a couple of Olympic buddies. All I had was a couple of beers, and then I said, "I've got to go see somebody about war surplus." But I felt very woozy driving to his place, and worse when I got there. I remember leaving, but nothing after that. What I discovered later was that I was so drunk that I blacked out and drove aimlessly through the Hollywood Hills. Finally I parked the car and got out to relieve myself against a tree before going to my apartment. But it wasn't my apartment and I ended up walking in circles for hours until I found my street. Before going out that night I'd put on a brand-new pair of shoes. The next morning, my heels were run-down.

When I woke up in the morning, I couldn't remember anything. And when I went outside I couldn't find my car. I reported it stolen. Two days later the police found it two miles away.

Another disappointment: I wanted to run again. There'd been no 1940 and 1944 Olympics, and it was a long time since I'd competed, but I decided to go for it for the 1948 games. I went down to the LA City College track to work out. I had to take it easy at first, but I worked hard and finally got in what I called good shape. Then I bore down, running for six weeks wearing heavy tennis shoes. When I thought I was ready I had Cynthia join me at the track. I gave her a stopwatch and asked her to call out my lap times. I settled into my starting stance and took off. I felt light. But when I passed Cynthia she called out "sixty-eight!" That couldn't be right. When I came around again she yelled, "two-seventeen." What? I couldn't be slowing down. So I pushed harder, and when I did I felt something go wrong in my ankle and searing pain in my calf. These were old injuries. I ignored them. But by the final lap I had nothing left. My trademark kick was gone. I collapsed on the infield grass. I'd run a 4:28. Way out of competition. Cynthia tried to be supportive, even weathered my anger, but she knew better.

My dream died there and then. In addition to all I'd been through, I became a victim of the war in the one pursuit that had always meant the most to me: running.

I had quit drinking to train. Now I had no reason to deny myself.

———

My USC buddy, Harry Read, and I cooked up a plan to take an adventure cruise. Harry had always had money, a beautiful car, and his own sailboat—a 34-foot yawl, the *Kummel*, which had unfortunately capsized in a hurricane off Lower California in 1936. His father owned lots of real estate, and his mother made sure Harry got a nice check every month.

Like all the athletes, I made a lot less money but I made up for it in having fun. I was an extra in movies like *The Hunchback of Notre Dame*, with Charles Laughton. I'm a street urchin. I still have the leotards they made me wear—but I stayed to the back of the scene because I didn't want anyone to see me in that getup. I also met Maureen O'Hara and got to dance with her at a party.

Now Harry had a 60-foot, two-masted schooner, the *Flyaway*. It needed work to be seaworthy and Harry paid for it to be refit for a voyage.

We replaced rotted planks on the starboard bow and fixed other woodwork. We bought a brand-new surplus landing barge—what the military used to get troops to shore—for $200. It had a 225-horsepower diesel motor, which we unhooked, hoisted out on a crane, and installed in the *Flyaway*. We repainted, varnished, and inspected every inch of the boat, and laid on new sails, a new refrigerator, and a new radio. We lashed on two fifty-gallon drums for reserve fuel.

As we worked I kept asking myself if I really wanted to make the trip. Why? I never actually liked being on the water—and that was *before* being stuck in a life raft for forty-seven days. On the other hand, we weren't going to sea ill-equipped, so maybe I was comparing apples and oranges.

Harry announced the trip in the newspapers. We couldn't handle the boat ourselves, so we advertised for crew members. The plan was to fish, hunt, and explore on the way to Acapulco. Under a big photo of the *Flyaway* in the *Pasadena Star News* ran the caption: "*WANT A VACATION? Harry Read, Eagle Rock sportsman, and Lou Zamperini, former USC national distance championship runner, are planning a leisure trip to romantic Acapulco in old Mejeeco . . . several berths are open and anybody wishing to make the jaunt may do so by getting in touch . . .*"

Another story said, "*A couple of intrepid amateur sailors undaunted by previous harrowing experiences at sea, are about to test their luck again . . .*"

A third cut right to the chase: "*Zamperini goes fishing. Takes two life rafts.*"

More than a few people wondered if I was crazy. Hadn't I had enough of the sea?

———

We got lots of interest, and chose a crew. Originally we wanted eight USC students, but we needed to share expenses and the students couldn't afford the $500 ante each. Instead we took on John Elliott, who in 1952 became the governor of American Samoa, and a businessman named Robinson. Another was the guy who inherited the Fisher Body Company—and he spoke a little Spanish. There was a gentleman with lots of money, and three others who managed to scrape together the fee. And a cook.

Lee Tracy, a Broadway and film actor, wanted to get away from his wife and come with us. We said yes, but then we heard from the Mexican consulate. "If you take Lee Tracy you will never enter Mexico. You won't be allowed to land."

"What? Why?"

Turned out that Tracy had recently been in Mexico City for a film directed by Howard Hawks. One day a military parade went by the hotel and a drunk Tracy went out on his balcony to watch. Then Tracy either urinated on the parade or maybe just returned an obscene gesture made by a Mexican standing in the street. Either way, Tracy had insulted Mexico, Mexicans, and the Mexican flag. Tracy was forced to leave Mexico and was replaced on the movie. We replaced Tracy on the boat with a 19-year-old kid from Long Beach named Steve.

THE PLAN WAS to take a shakedown cruise to train the mostly green crew, and to eliminate those who couldn't adjust physically or mentally to the discipline and rough life of sailing. They needed to learn the handling characteristics of the ship, to become familiar with the pitch and yaw of the *Flyaway*, to learn the sailor's jargon, the name and function of each sail. But in order to make our announced departure date, we scrubbed the shakedown. Harry filled two padded and insulated five-gallon containers with layers of dry ice and steaks. We loaded up with fresh water, beer, fruit and vegetables, bottled goods and lots of distilled spirits, and sailed out of San Pedro, just south of Los Angeles, on the afternoon of Sunday, February 8. We stopped first at Ensenada, two hundred miles south, where we discovered that Harry had forgotten to fill one of the spare diesel fuel tanks. Also, the cook complained of nausea all the way down, and he nibbled only on bread and vegetables, like a pantry mouse. Hardly an auspicious beginning, especially for the guy who was supposed to prepare our meals.

We went ashore in shifts and headed directly for Hussong's Cantina for tequila and beer. A few drinks later, Harry had to take a leak but there was only one toilet and a long line. Harry had followed some locals who were relieving themselves at the curb outside and did the same, when two policemen grabbed him and took him off to jail. I followed closely behind. They tossed him into the cell and when he saw a great big rat come through a hole in the wall, Harry started screaming: "Louie! Get me outta here!"

The police said we had to wait for the judge. "When's the judge going to get here?" I asked.

"Oh, maybe one, two, three, four days." I could hear Harry screaming again.

I figured it was a racket so I asked, "How much is the bail?"

"Ten dollars."

So simple. I gave them ten dollars and Harry got out.

———

WE SAILED ANOTHER 270 miles to Cedros Island, about half-way down the Baja Peninsula.

When we anchored, two locals in a rowboat approached. They had lobster for sale. We bought twenty for twenty-five cents each, and two lemons. A couple of hours later they came back with a pile of coconuts. We gave them gifts for their families, and they came back *again*, this time with buckets of lobsters, which they tossed on the deck. Dinner was terrific.

We managed to find 100 gallons of syrupy, low-grade diesel about forty miles away in Puerto San Bartolomé and then set course for the approximately 500-mile sail to Cabo San Lucas, where I sent a telegram to Cynthia telling her all was well.

On the way, I was also looking forward to visiting the

Tres Marias Islands (Isla Maria Madre, Isla Maria Magdalena, Isla Maria Cleofas), about sixty-two miles off the coast, between Mazatlan and Puerto Vallarta, and 250 miles or so from Cabo.

The first stop was Maria Madre, site of a large prison camp. The Mexican government was quite proud of the prison, built in 1905, but at the time it was a feared place, full of violence, disease, and forced labor. It was also supposed to be escape-proof—the Alcatraz of Mexico—but turned out to be more porous than expected.

The seas had been surprisingly calm so we motored into the island's harbor. By moonlight we could see a large two-story building and a pier. We anchored at 9 p.m. Shortly afterward, a rowboat pulled up with three men. We asked them to board and come below. One was a lieutenant from the army barracks that provided security for the prison; another, his sidekick. The third, their oarsman, was a prisoner and stayed on deck. They were pleasant and we shared Canadian Club and cigarettes. I cooked them a T-bone steak and fried potatoes. Tears came to their eyes because it had been a very long time since they'd had such good food. We didn't expect that kind of reaction.

I took the oarsman some food and a pack of cigarettes, and they rowed back to the island.

We were up at 6 a.m., lowered the outboard, and went ashore. One guard stood on the dock. Some of the locals tried to sell us souvenirs and sundries, and we said we'd buy later. A ragged, unshaven, but well-tanned man, probably in his early 30s, approached. He spoke good English, which made sense because he was an American who'd gotten in trouble in Mexico City just after the war started. "My name's Dan," he said. "Prisoner number 5005. They call me Dirty Dan." Again, obvious. "My time is up in four months."

Dan showed us around. The island was run by a state official who was both the governor and the chief judge. He lived in a beautiful mansion. The prisoners lived in a collection of "fishing villages." In other words, no cells with bars. It was more Papillon than Alacatraz—unless you were uncooperative.

We invited the governor, the prison officials, and the officers in charge back to the *Flyaway* for lunch. At their request Dan came as the interpreter, and sat with us during the meal.

After a couple of Vat 69s and sodas, we fed them our best steaks, Waldorf salad, canned spaghetti, green string beans, lemon Jell-O, and coffee. Appetizers consisted of cherries, pickles, salami, Ritz and soda crackers, and dates. Dan told us that the governor was quite thoughtful. "He's new to the island and has done much for the prisoners, and is now trying to do much more." Dan was smart. And canny. The governor patted Dan on the back and talked and laughed with us as he would with old buddies.

We were invited to dine the next evening at the governor's

home, the large building we had seen in the moonlight when we first moored. Drinks and dinner promptly at 6 p.m. We all combed our hair and shaved. They served us Bacardi rum and Pepsi with lime. Steve played boogie-woogie on the governor's spinet.

Then Dan brought a long, narrow box to the verandah. He opened it and a nine-foot boa slithered out. A prison officer picked it up and put it around his neck, then passed it on to someone else. I looked at its muscular body contracting back and forth. When I was offered a turn at holding the snake, I declined.

After dinner we told the governor that we were setting off for Isla Magdalena in a few hours, to hunt. "They're short on food," he said, and asked if we'd mind delivering 1,000 pounds of corn. We agreed. He also said two of his officials could go with us to lead the hunt.

We shoved off at midnight and ninety minutes later were at Isla Magdalena. Though it was the middle of the night, the two officials who'd come with us started yelling: "Antonio! Antonio!" Seems they wanted Antonio to row out and get them—and the corn. We joined in. "Antonio! Antonio!" After twenty minutes a dugout canoe with a single man pulled up broadside. He loaded two sacks of corn and took one of the officials—leaving the other to watch the rest of the corn. They said they would return at 5 a.m. to go hunting.

Antonio came back as promised and a couple of men began off-loading the corn while we went ashore. Antonio explained that the island had an abundance of key deer, small even when fully grown. I had my high-powered .30-40 Krag, but to get the key deer all you need is a .22 rifle. I had two.

Antonio introduced us to his wife and their three little kids half dangling from her arms and legs, and then we men split into two groups. Harry, Steve, and I went with one of the guards from Maria Madre, and Elliott and a guy named Johnstone went with Antonio. We hiked about three miles but saw no deer. Steve and I watched by a water hole while Harry and the guard took off. Again, no thirsty deer, so we kept moving. After another mile we spotted Antonio and Elliott working the crest of a hill, and climbed to meet them.

Then everyone spotted the same deer. I leveled my gun as one of the prison guards raised his. I waited for him to fire first, but he hesitated, so I aimed for the shoulder and pulled the trigger. The deer rolled about fifty feet to the stream. It was a small doe. I gutted it on the spot and Antonio tied its legs and slung it over his shoulder.

Antonio's wife made us coffee and eggs. We gave them the deer and several doves we'd also bagged. I also gave Antonio one of my .22s and five hundred bullets.

So far the trip had gone well. But the poverty we encountered in the Tres Marias Islands, their meager supplies and primitive conditions, were surprising and upsetting. It was easy to forget how good we had it in the United States and how poorly some of the rest of the world lived. We gave whoever we encountered portions of our supplies and were unexpectedly, but happily, as much humanitarians as sportsmen and adventurers.

We all got in the dinghy, said farewell to Antonio, and headed back to the *Flyaway*. We motored to the other side of the island and raised the sails. The wind was sharp—and so was our new crew member, a parrot that Antonio had gifted to us in exchange for the deer. We named the bird Hogan. But every time someone moved on deck the damn parrot spit out a line of squawks and yells that would put a holy roller speaking in tongues to shame. When we got close to him he snapped at us with his little beak.

The wind was good and smooth and we were enjoying the sail on a beautiful afternoon when the boom and the main sheet swung quickly from one side to the other, and Hogan was damn near thrown over the rail. Harry watched, agape, at the wheel while the rest of us laughed as the parrot clawed and dug in his talons for life. Then we hit a large ground swell. Hogan's grip failed and he went sailing over the rail squawking all the way.

Once in the water, Hogan flapped his wings desperately to keep afloat. Johnstone and I lowered the dinghy. Steve, who had taken an immediate liking to the bird, came running up and wouldn't let anyone else man the boat. He climbed into the dinghy in a hurry while we towed it, but he didn't lie flat enough and the dinghy capsized from the boat's wake. Steve hung on, swallowing a bit of water, while Harry made a pass at him. I was on the bow giving directions. On the next pass Johnstone and I both shouted out directions while Harry came within ten yards of Steve. We could easily have swung broadside, but Harry—who was a nice guy on land, but could be officious and arrogant at sea—never listened to us.

We made the next pass for the parrot. I swung from the bow on a chain. I caught the bird but was unable to hold him. Johnstone had better luck. Then we got Steve. I grabbed the dinghy line and handed it to Johnstone, who pulled Steve aboard. Steve was cold and in shock. His stomach took a while to settle as he lay in a bunk below.

Once safe and dry, Hogan began to butt heads with Harry. They quickly became mortal enemies. Hogan really liked to squawk—maybe that's why we got him as a "gift"—and Harry hated it. He kept trying to smack the bird to shut him up. Harry caught a few feathers but mostly missed. From then on, whenever Harry walked by, Hogan would try to peck him. Harry was furious. He treated the bird like a human being, saying, "Shut up! I'm the skipper!" Hogan responded by trying to nip him again. The rest of us got a kick out of the discord. Hogan wouldn't take any crap from anybody. He wouldn't back down. I think Harry secretly respected Hogan because they had so much in common. In his dreams, Harry probably pictured Hogan instigating a mutiny and taking command of the ship. Hogan had my vote.

————

WE MADE A quick stop in Puerto Vallarta for more fuel, and took in the February 24 Dia de Bandera, or Flag Day, parade, courtesy of the mayor. Then we set a course for Acapulco.

This time we didn't need the motor. The wind became fresher and fresher, until we had to haul in the light jib. Steve was at the helm but, after a couple of minutes, he looked rigid and pale. Harry made me take over. Steve was a fast learner for someone so young, but with the wind pushing and the seas rising we needed experience.

I struggled with the heavy seas for a couple of hours, and then got some sleep. I awoke too soon to a great heaving and twisting. Swells tossed the *Flyaway* this way and that— and then out of nowhere it felt as if we were hit with a hundred angry cannonballs. It was as if Neptune had risen from the sea to impale us with his trident again and again. We were in the middle of a white squall, a *tabasco*. It slapped our starboard side and the boat was pelted—no, smothered—in heavy winds and a violent rain.

We had no time to batten down the hatches or bring down the sails. The mainsail was ripping but we could do little about it while trying to keep our balance and not be tossed overboard. Waves broke over the boat. The main cabin took on a foot of water and shorted out the electrical power system. Now we couldn't start the engine. The bilge pumps stopped and the icebox quit. And the radio was gone. We'd been in regular contact with the Coast Guard, and I realized that we wouldn't be able to check in.

Try as I could to hold the tiller, I was losing the battle. Then I felt a terrifically hard knock on the tiller shaft. I thought it was one of our large gas cans banging around in the lazarette, where the steering gear is located through a hatch underneath the aft deck. Steve hollered and Harry came over. I moved the tiller to try for a better heading, but it swung freely and was useless. Harry dived into the hatch.

While the boat swayed, rolled, and broached waves, Harry discovered the trouble. The force of the storm had sheered the heavy ¾-inch bolt on the steering universal joint, leaving us adrift and unable to steer.

I called all hands on deck and rang the hell out of the bell. Harry ordered the jib down immediately as it was slack, swinging back and forth, and would be torn to shreds in another thirty seconds. He ordered the main staysail and forward staysail changed at such a pitch that they would allow us to keep pretty close to our course without rudder control and without hitting a wave broadside and turning turtle.

Harry was far calmer at this critical moment than he ever was in lowering a dinghy. He didn't lose his head and had remarkable aptitude.

The last thing I wanted was to be in trouble on the ocean again.

I hung on to the useless tiller while Harry scrounged around for something, anything, that could replace the bolt for the steering joint. It took him nearly ten minutes before he found a substitute bolt, and another five minutes to get it aligned and shoved through the holes. I was finally able to put the ship into a heading that minimized our exposure.

Our crew was too green to be of much help. They could bail water, and did, but otherwise they were petrified. The life raft was all tangled up. We were driven out to sea. The motor wouldn't start. The sails were shredding. We just had to reel in and tie down what we could, relax, and wait for the mercy of the sea. (Later, when we hauled in the mainsail, we discovered a one-foot tear in the upper quarter. All the buttons were snapped and the pockets around them shredded.)

Hogan, meanwhile, weaved and swayed and made very little noise, which was a relief from his usual chatter and complaints. And then he lost his footing, went overboard, and we never saw him again. I, for one, missed him. Now who would keep Harry honest?

I stayed on the tiller riding out the seas. I sent Steve below to make sure the toilet window was closed. It wasn't, and water was pouring in. We checked the bilge. It was full of water and running into the staterooms.

———

THE STORM PASSED but the sea remained rough all night. My sleeping bag, with me in it, was tossed to the floor more than once. But we managed to ride out the worst of it, and in the morning . . . the sea was like glass. Absolutely no wind anywhere. We were grateful. We were also lost, pushed miles out to sea, with torn sails and no power. The *tabasco* had shorted our radio, saturated our sleeping bags. Below decks looked like a crime scene. Twelve of our fourteen water glasses were broken.

We immediately knew that we wouldn't be at our next port of call on schedule. The Coast Guard, whom we'd kept informed of our progress, would worry—and maybe try to find us. That, in turn, would distress our families if we were missing for long enough.

"Are you scared?" Steve asked me.

"What do you mean?"

"After what happened in the war? Drifting for days."

"No, no. Not at all," I said. I wanted to inspire confidence and calm, but I wasn't lying, either. What I didn't say was that because we were so well stocked with fuel and food and drink, I could probably last forty-seven years—not that I wanted to encourage the idea. At any rate, keeping the crew on an even mental keel was a role that I was used to, and good for the soul.

———————

I TOOK ON two repair tasks. One was to hang over the rail in a sling, with a hand drill, and bore some holes in the sides just above the deck line, to drain the water. The other was to sew and patch the sails, which I did with a baseball stitch. The others cleaned below and secured everything.

Otherwise, we were stuck waiting for the wind. We decided to go swimming and rigged the halyard so that we could swing ourselves out and, at the highest point, let go into the water. We took turns plummeting into the smooth sea with the most graceful trajectory we could manage, always being aware of the possibility of sharks. We swung and dove and swam naked. Steve ended up with a sunburnt penis.

We still had a good supply of food and water aboard. Also lots of liquor. Cases of Canadian Club, crème de cacao. That called for drinks. We cut the tops off of coconuts, fortified the milk with vodka or gin, and added fresh-squeezed lime— to ward off scurvy, of course. We also had a sack full of live langouste. We boiled these spiny lobsters in a deck bucket then dipped the tender and tasty morsels in a coffee can of hot salted butter melted by the sun. Yes, we worked to restore the boat, but otherwise we had nothing to do but party and wait for some wind. What a way to live.

———

WE MUST HAVE been drifting slightly toward the coast because, although we could not see land, we could finally smell it. Harry and I redoubled our efforts to start the motor, which we'd painstakingly dried as best we could. We'd done the same to the electrical components and radio. After careful examination and a thorough process of elimination, we agreed that the problem with the engine was that the intake jets were the wrong size for the heavy fuel we picked up at Puerto Vallarta. We changed to larger jets, and the engine somewhat reluctantly came to life, as did other equipment.

We set a course for Puerto Vallarta, where we effected more repairs and restored the radio. We'd been drifting for almost a week. I got a message to my wife describing our predicament and assuring her I was all right. Later, I would get a letter she'd sent chiding me for being selfishly out of touch for a whole week. But another letter quickly followed saying that she understood what had happened and would I please ignore what she'd written.

We arrived in Acapulco in early March. The inner bay was aglow with ship lights. The encircling hills were dotted with homes and a few hotels.

While motoring slowly toward the yacht club, De Yatez, we heard a yell from a nearby schooner. It was Lee Lewis from the *Adelia*, who told us to anchor up next to him. He had already been in Acapulco for fifteen days. Lee and crew came aboard and gave us all the dope on the place. "It's not too expensive," he said, "but good chow is scarce. Nightlife starts at ten p.m."

We went to the best hotel first, the Casablanca, then the Hotel Americas, where we made a beeline for the outdoor bar that served drinks in hollowed-out pineapples. The whole joint was surrounded by a ten-foot bamboo fence. When we finished our drinks, the bartender told us to toss the pineapples over the fence where the locals waited for the shells.

This was our routine. Beach by day, hotel life by night. On the third night we went back to the Hotel Americas bar but found the lobby leading to the bar and pool area closed. Two bulky security guards forbid anyone to enter.

We peeked past them and saw a large private party in progress behind closed glass doors. "Whose party is it?" I asked one guard.

"Virginia Hill's," he said, blankly. He had no idea who she was, but I did. Virginia was Bugsy Siegel's girlfriend. And I do mean *was*. Bugsy had since been assassinated.

I asked the guard to take a note to Virginia and she came running out. After a big hug she said, "Louie, come on in!"

"There are six of us," I said.

"If they're your friends, they're all welcome," she said.

———

THE NEXT DAY, March 7, I got a telegram from Cynthia. *"Your presence is urgently needed come home at once."* Now what? I felt that old sinking feeling in the pit of my stomach.

I caught a flight for Los Angeles; Harry and the crew stayed behind. When I got home, I got the bad news: Remember the D8 Caterpillars deal I'd gotten involved in when I gave our Hawaiian middleman $7,000 to hold the machines?

Our contact had spent the money on himself and his family. I'd lost everything.

And yet, not long after, Cynthia also had good news: She was pregnant. (Our daughter, Cynthia—known as Cissy—was born on January 7, 1949.)

———

As I'd PREDICTED, when the Coast Guard hadn't heard from us they got worried. They triangulated our supposed position with weather reports and figured we'd gone down in the squall. Thanks to my cabling Cynthia before leaving Puerto Vallarta for the second time, she knew I was all right. When contacted by the Associated Press, she said, "He certainly isn't lost, and he'll be home in a few days." That story ran on March 7, 1948, the day she cabled me to come home immediately.

———

Is THERE A moral to this postwar slice-of-my-life adventure story? Maybe more than one. First, a fool and his money are soon parted. Second, you can't run away from your problems and responsibilities, because they'll be waiting for you when you get back—no matter how much fun you have in the meantime. Once I got home I slipped back into my old ways, and with the added responsibility of a child looming, I grew more desperate.

And third, don't tick off the parrot.

# Don't Leave the Crucial Details to Others

Not long after I got back from my sailing trip along the Mexican coastline, I went missing again. I didn't plan it. I promise. But this time, I didn't make the headlines either because I used a phony name to avoid attention.

A FAMOUS DENTIST in those days, with office branches up and down the West Coast, had a crazy son, Tommy, who was a fraternity brother of Harry Read's—the skipper of the *Flyaway*—and mine. He told us that he wanted to go to Catalina. He had it all worked out. "Sailing is too slow," he said. "So I'll make you a deal. You're close to the girls at the Earl Carroll Theater—the most beautiful girls in the world. I'll get my dad's twin-engine cabin cruiser if you bring some girls."

"Okay," I said, after I asked my wife, Cynthia, and got her blessing. She knew how much I loved Catalina—though usually we sailed there on Harry's boat and spent time with a group of actors and actresses.

I did know some of the performers at the Earl Carroll Theater, and a few of them would certainly enjoy a fun day off. "Gas up the boat, put plenty of drinks and food aboard, and I'll bring three girls," I said.

The Earl Carroll Theater was at 6230 Sunset Boulevard, just east of Vine Street. (Later it became the Moulin Rouge, the Hullabaloo, the Kaleidoscope, the Aquarius Theater, the Longhorn Theater, the Chevy Chase Theater, and the production facility of the Nickelodeon Channel called Nickelodeon on Sunset.) The theater had opened in 1938 and included technical innovations like a stage with a huge, two-section revolving turntable in the middle that allowed each ring to revolve at different speeds at the same time in the same or opposite directions, an elevator to bring performers up from beneath the stage, three swings that lowered from the auditorium ceiling, a revolving staircase, and a rain machine. Out front was a twenty-foot-high painting of Carroll's girlfriend Beryl Wallace. There was also a Wall of Fame, which preserved in cement the personal inscriptions to Earl Carroll of more than one hundred and fifty of Hollywood's most glamorous stars.

Earl was an extraordinary showman. A partial guest list for opening night on December 26, 1938: Clark Gable and Carole Lombard, Marlene Dietrich, Tyrone Power, Sonja Henie, Bob Hope, Betty Grable, Jack Benny, Claudette Colbert, Robert Taylor, Constance Bennett, Daryl Zanuck, Franchot Tone, Errol Flynn, David O. Selznick, Louis B. Mayer, Dolores del Rio, Edgar Bergen, Jack Warner, W. C. Fields, Don Ameche, Walter Pidgeon, and Jimmy Durante.

Carroll's motto/boast: "Through these portals pass the most beautiful girls in the world." And it was true.

After the show, I went back to the bar and out came the girls. I was in uniform. I quickly found three young ladies happy to take a day trip to Catalina. Two were solo dancers and one was part of the ensemble. One had been dating Mark C. Bloome, the tire magnate.

Earl said, "Louis, these gals have got to be back for tomorrow night's show."

"We're leaving early in the morning and we can be in Catalina in thirty minutes on this boat," I said. "We'll be back early. Don't worry about it."

———

THE NEXT MORNING we met in San Pedro, had breakfast, and took off. We wanted to keep our promise about getting back in time. With the twin-screw engine pumping I stood on the deck and let the cool salt air wash over me as we shot through the water. "Oh man," I said to Harry. "I can't wait to get to Catalina."

I'd have to. About halfway there we ran out of gas. One minute we were on deck having fun, taking turns driving the boat, and the next minute, we were sputtering. I had failed to take my own advice to be prepared, and hadn't thought to check the gas gauge. We'd depended on Tommy to be responsible. Big mistake.

Dead in the water, the boat started to pitch a bit on the waves. The girls were nauseated and Harry went below to find something to settle their stomachs. Instead, he discovered that Tommy had forgotten to stock the boat with food or drink. Harry did find some stale crackers, and an old ginger ale bottle three-quarters full of water—with a cigarette butt someone had thoughtfully dropped in.

The radio didn't work, either.

Boy did we give it to Tommy. What a slipshod, totally irresponsible guy.

We drifted for hours. The girls were below, where the boat rocked the least, trying not to lose their breakfasts. Finally, a big vessel came by. We waved our shirts at it. They pulled alongside real slow.

"What's your problem?"

"We ran out of gas!"

That's when the girls came up. They'd heard us talking. Imagine the captain of the other boat watching two blondes and one brunette, all long-legged dancers, appear from below. They were beautiful. They had outstanding figures.

"Jesus!" he snapped. "What is this? Some kind of gag? You guys can go to hell." And he took off.

Soon, we had drifted as far as Catalina, which lay a few miles east. Harry said that if we put him overboard in the dinghy, he'd row in and get help.

We didn't hear from Harry again, and by the next morning we were beyond Catalina. I needed a plan. I went below and got the mirror from the bathroom, took it on deck, and waited, hoping a plane would fly over. One eventually did and I gave it an S-O-S. The pilot saw and came circling down. He could see we were out there plopping around and had to believe our S-O-S was serious. Next thing I knew he dropped a long ribbon attached to a package. Inside were malt tablets and some gum. Big survival kit! He'd also included a note: "Promise to give me the phone numbers of the three girls and I'll send for help."

I flashed out O-K, O-K, O-K with the mirror. Before long the sky was full of planes—or at least it seemed that way. Later, I found out that he'd relayed in a message: "Three beautiful girls with long hair. . . ." Who would come to our rescue otherwise? The aircraft all kept diving as low as they could to take a look at the girls. One of the planes just skimmed our nonfunctioning radio aerial. The girls did their bit, though, standing on deck, waving at the pilots as they flew by.

Then we saw the Coast Guard ship. "Look," I told everyone. "I've been missing so many times. The newspapers will make fun of me. Please, please don't tell them my name.

I'm going to give them a false name, my uncle's name: Louis Dossi."

Everyone agreed. The Coast Guard pulled up and threw a line. We all went aboard, and I carried out my little deception. Before long we were all in Avalon, with Tommy's cabin cruiser towed in as well.

But what about Harry? Turns out he'd made it ashore—but on the deserted end of Catalina. He'd had to hike to get to Avalon, where he'd alerted the Coast Guard.

We gassed up the cabin cruiser and got back to the mainland as quickly as we could. I'd also taken the name, address, and phone number of the first pilot, and I kept my word, sending him the girls' names and the phone number of Earl Carroll's.

Carroll was madder than a hornet, but we never got to settle the situation. On June 17, 1948, he and Beryl Wallace died in an airplane crash.

Is there a lesson here? Sure. Don't leave the crucial details to someone you don't know—especially when your life may depend on it.

And: There's rarely a situation that a pretty woman can't help fix.

# There's Always an Answer to Everything

*Meeting Cynthia's plane at Burbank Airport, 1945.*
*A few weeks later we were married. In 1949,*
*her love and faith lit the path to my rebirth.*

# You Need a Cloud to
# Have a Silver Lining

I survived the war, but then I had to survive *myself* coming home from the war. Despite the good times and all the attention, I was under a cloud that kept growing darker. I had nightmares about killing the Bird from which I woke up shouting and sweating. My running legs were gone and I couldn't compete anymore, which broke my heart. I wanted to strike it rich, but lost money instead. I drank and fought. I knew I was on the wrong path—but didn't know what to do about it.

This situation was especially troubling because I'd always been an optimist, figuring I'd find a way through my troubles—which I usually did. But now I'd lost my positive attitude. I felt entitled, put upon, and that life was unfair. I was confused, frustrated, and desperate. I couldn't blame myself so I blamed God, in whom I believed, but didn't otherwise think about. I'd forgotten my promise to Him on the raft that I must have made ten thousand times.

I remember driving my wife down Hollywood Boulevard one day and getting into an altercation with a guy in the crosswalk ahead of me. He had slowed down for what I thought was no reason. I didn't brake, and just barely missed him. As I passed on his left, he turned and spit. It hit my wife's window. I screeched to a stop and confronted him. I was just going to beat the hell out of him when Cynthia shouted, "No, Louis, no! Please! Don't do it! Don't do it!" So I let go of him and shoved him away, and got back in the car.

Another time, in Newport Beach, I was walking into a bar with my buddies. A big guy shoved the door and knocked me back. He had forty pounds on me. The beach was right there, so I got him out on the sand. I knew I had to dance around him until he got tired. Sure enough, that's what happened. Once he got winded, I pummeled him with punches until he went down.

I couldn't stop hating. And worse, my marriage to Cynthia had reached a breaking point. I was cruel to her in public. At home, belongings were tossed and dishes broken. One afternoon she stopped me just before I shook the baby because she wouldn't stop crying. I was out of my mind.

Cynthia took Cissy and went to Florida to see her mother and explain the situation. She came back determined to get a divorce. She said it was hopeless. Cynthia had every right to complain. We were partners and I kept acting alone. I was angry. Depressed. Erratic. I didn't have a steady income. I got taken by different people because I was always sure that, "This is going to be the deal." All my life they'd called me "Lucky Louis." But everything failed, one after the other. I may have kept in shape but I was also drunk every night. I just didn't let others see it—though I'm sure they had their suspicions. But I couldn't hide my distress and dissolution from my family.

A neighbor couple knew we were in distress and tried to get us to go to hear a new evangelist speak. I wanted nothing to do with it. I knew I was a rotten failure. An evil stinker. I knew that everything about me was wrong, but when the subject of religion came up, I couldn't bear it.

Cynthia decided to go anyway, with our neighbors. I said, "Okay, as long as I don't have to go, she can go." I loved Cynthia, but I knew we were going to get a divorce anyway, so what did it matter?

When Cynthia got home, she seemed to glow. She was so enthusiastic about what she'd heard and experienced that she announced she would not seek a divorce. I was relieved. But then she began to press me to go with her the next time. She was certain that what I'd hear might be the solution to my problems. I still did not want to bend.

Cynthia finally persuaded me to go because she said the preacher would talk a lot about science. I loved science. Still, it took about a week to get me to downtown Los Angeles. We drove with our neighbors because I'd lost my car as collateral on a loan I couldn't pay back. I stood outside the tent entrance studying the preacher's picture. He held an open Bible in one hand and seemed like a serious young man. Otherwise, he was hardly my picture of an evangelist, and my impression was confirmed inside when, after some hymns, the young man walked purposefully onstage.

Tall, handsome, clean-cut, athletic, Billy Graham had clear blue eyes and seemed even younger in person than in his photograph. He stood erect, shoulders squared. It was early October, and the place was packed. In fact, Graham's stay had been extended from three weeks to eight—not bad for his first major outing.

Halfway through his sermon, I got mad. When I heard that everyone was a sinner, I got defensive. I knew I was, but I didn't need him to remind me. I walked out.

By the way, the sermon had nothing to do with science.

Cynthia worked on me all the next day, trying to convince me to go back. I finally gave in—for her—and said, "Okay, I'll go back, but under the condition that when he says 'Every head bowed and every eye closed,' we get out." She agreed.

The next time, there was again no mention of science— only sin. And it seemed directed right at me. My confusion and guilt were overwhelming. And yet I couldn't stop listening. Every time I raised an objection in my mind, Graham seemed to sense it and answered me.

When I heard the agreed-upon trigger words I grabbed Cynthia's hand and stood to leave. I squeezed along the row between knees and chair backs on my way to the center aisle. But at the same time I couldn't stop thinking about my promises—and I hesitated. I knew what I should do, but I didn't want to do it. I was afraid. And for that, I felt ashamed of myself. But when I reached the aisle I could no longer resist. I just let my instinct take over and instead of leaving I went forward.

Turning toward the stage was the crucial moment, the fork in the road. At the stage I fell to my knees, emotionally overcome. I asked for forgiveness and invited Christ into my life.

Although I now believe that my life had unfolded according to God's plan, at the time I was as good as thinking: If you're there and you can help me, I am ready to accept your help because I am out of options. I've tried everything else I can think of. Nothing has worked.

I had nothing left to lose.

That admission itself was the beginning of my recovery. I'd always known that I'd come home from the war with a problem, but I had never been willing to ask for help—from anyone.

But now I had, and my whole body and spirit felt different. Wonderful. Calm. Free. I wanted to keep feeling that way. My life of training and commitment to a goal kicked in.

I wanted to survive and somehow I knew that to maintain this sudden inner peace I would have to give up the habits I'd developed that weren't working. I was willing to give it my all.

---

I've often been asked what that moment of transformation feels like. Epiphany, revelation, call it what you want: It's different for everyone. But for me . . . I felt weightless. Suddenly calm. I was no longer fighting myself. And my burdens lifted.

When I was racing, I had no idea in advance if I'd run great or poorly, if I'd win or lose. And this even though I won often. Each time I'd get a major attack of butterflies as I walked out onto the track. I was actually more anxious when running against Glenn Cunningham and other great runners than I was approaching my first enemy target during the war. The only way to deal with the anxiety was to accept that it would always be there—and to remember that as soon as the starting gun went off I was 100 percent committed, and on automatic pilot. My training took hold and only one question remained to be answered: *How am I going to survive this race and win?*

That's what I experienced on my knees. Butterflies. And the questions: What am I doing? Can I do it? Can I survive this new challenge? The moments before I turned toward the

stage on which Billy Graham stood felt like the seconds before a race. Whatever was going to happen, I wanted to get
it over with. I wanted to stop waiting in the starting blocks.
In a race the starter says, "On your mark, get set . . ." and if
he holds that "get set" just a tiny bit too long, your already
tense muscles tense more, but you can't move. It really makes
you uptight.

I just wanted the starter to shoot the gun so that my training could take over.

The revelation was that I had to be the starter.

————

In a daze, yet relieved, I was led to a prayer room behind
the curtain. I spoke quietly to a counselor. He said that I
needed to "stick with the Lord" and not try to stand alone
any longer—a tough requirement since most of my life I had
depended only on myself. He also made it clear that I was
just at the beginning, and that the act of changing my life
had been just one moment. I would face many challenges in
the moments and days to come—a situation that is hardly
exclusive to faith-based transformations. Think of the doctor saying "Quit smoking or you'll die." Transitions are un-
balancing. Cautionary. Disorienting. I was told that I'd be
tempted by my old ways and have doubts. "You're like a
child. It's not unusual for negative influences to appear just
after a conversion, saying, 'What you did was a lot of balo-

ney.' Your friends might question you and think you've gone off the deep end. But the more you get into it, the stronger your roots will grow."

Soon, I found Cynthia waiting in the audience and she threw her arms around me. I looked at her and knew in my heart, as if it had always been so, that I was through drinking, through smoking, through with everything. My lifelong desire for revenge had evaporated. I didn't know what the future held—would I be rich, poor, whatever?—but that didn't matter. "I'm through with my past life," I told Cynthia. "I'm through."

I believed I had found what would work for me.

———

WHEN WE GOT home I immediately poured all my liquor down the drain, though not a three-hundred-year-old bottle of cognac that my father-in-law, an importer, had given us. I simply returned it. I threw my cigarettes in the garbage.

When I awoke the next morning I was stunned to realize that I hadn't dreamed about the Bird. And to this day I haven't. In fact, I forgave him because the ability to forgive is a major result of my transformation. Imagine your doctor cutting out the hating part of your personality. I still remember the facts, of course, but since then the violent emotions are gone. I had clung to the idea that hating the Bird was the same as getting even, but I knew then that whoever I hated didn't know my feelings, and could not be hurt. I only hurt myself.

———

THE DAYS TO come brought the predicted challenges. For example, parties. Remember, I'd come home from the war and Hollywood had opened itself to me. Every night we'd go out. There were free dinners and drinks. I took full advantage. But now I wouldn't drink, even though my buddies, who didn't understand the nature of how I'd changed, urged me to join in.

I'd say, "No way," and was so enthusiastic about my new life that I'd eagerly try to explain it in a jumble of words.

I remember being at the home of a man who'd invented backache pills. I was sitting on the floor talking to a group of actresses who had flocked around me because they'd all listened to Billy Graham, and they knew that he'd made big headlines in the Hearst papers because of three men who had come forward: me, Jim Vaus (the gangster Mickey Cohen's wiretapper), and Stuart Hamblen (one of radio's first singing cowboys). But the host's sons kept picking on me: "C'mon, hey, Louis, you won't last two weeks." I finally went to the kitchen and told the host, "Well, I did what I could do." I thanked him for the party and went home.

The next day the host called me to apologize. He said,

"When you left, several of the guys said, 'Man, I wish I could do what Zamperini did.'"

His call gave me new strength and vigor. I'd learned something important. I decided to preach less and instead just live my life as an example of my faith so that anyone could tell the difference between the past and present.

These moments were tests. I had friends who actually watched me for a year to see if I was just acting. My buddies said, "He can't stick it out, not with everything he's done."

After a year, when they saw that I was still on my new path and seemed much happier, they started to believe me that change was possible. Harry Read was one. He finally came forward himself, and told me, "I just wasn't sure, Louis. Knowing you the way I do, I just couldn't believe it. But I've watched you, and believe you're sincere."

———

The Bible warns that a smooth sea never made a good sailor. I'm sure all faiths express their own version of this tenet. Nothing happens overnight. The picture painted by the well-meaning and overenthusiastic is that after a conversion God gives the new believer a steady diet of happiness and nothing can go wrong. That's not true. On the contrary, like every other sincere person who is striving to believe in a new way of life—however they get there—in spite of having so long lived another way, with a mind conditioned to cynicism,

I had to go through a period of despondency, doubt, and painful self-examination. Deep meanings aren't immediately revealed because, frankly, like trying to teach calculus to a second-grader, you're not able to handle it. I remember once hearing a man brag, "Ever since I became a Christian, my life's been a bowl of cherries." I turned to him and said, "You know what you need? You need Christ." In other words, a dose of humility and reality.

All major changes take daily work. It's not happy magic all the time.

———

Cynthia was stronger than I was, faith-wise. Her support was a big help in my early days when I made my conversion public, and was up against doubters and naysayers. She would always say, "Have faith. God, in his own time, will work things out."

And, I have to tell the truth for me, they always did seem to work out.

# Know When You've Done All You Can Do

_____

I once spoke at a church and a couple who attended regularly got up and walked out after twenty minutes. After the service was over the pastor called them and asked, "Why did you walk out?"

"We come to church to hear about Jesus," they said. "We heard about the war. We didn't hear about Jesus."

"You should have waited until the end of the talk," he said.

Another time, I spoke at an Optimist International meeting—an association of almost three thousand clubs around the world dedicated to "Bringing Out the Best in Kids"—and this time mentioned Christianity to start with. A man stood up and said, "I didn't come here to be preached to," and he walked out.

Oh, well.

I tell my story just as it happened: I'm a rascal, I'm in trouble, I'm an athlete, I'm in the war, I'm in trouble, I'm a

POW, I come home. I fall apart. And then as I near the climax I know people are asking themselves, "I wonder what's coming next?" I tell them about what happened, but I don't preach.

———————

I used to struggle with my own eagerness.

Back in the prop airplane days of 1957, I was in Chicago, waiting for a plane. My flight was overbooked and the airline wanted volunteers to give up their seats. They called my name. At the desk I said, "Look, I've got a meeting tonight in Oakland and I cannot miss that flight."

I returned to my seat. The guy next to me said, "Oh, so you're Louis Zamperini?"

"I am," I said.

Then he heard his name on the PA. I knew it; he was a famous tennis player. "I can't let them bounce me," he said, as he stood. "I've got to be in Hawaii tomorrow at noon."

We sat around waiting to board and my mind got to working. Oh boy, this famous tennis player, I'd love to win him for the Lord.

Wrong idea. Self-serving. I just wanted to get the glory and the credit because he was well-known.

We ended up next to each other on the plane and I started talking. He clammed up. I felt terrible. I grabbed a magazine and pretended to read it while I prayed silently to myself: Boy,

I really messed this up. I'm sorry, I was just overbearing. I'm not going to say another word to him, not another word; he'll have to do the talking.

For thirty minutes I just sat there. Finally, he turned to me and said, "Louis, there's one thing that's always bothered me about the Bible." I forget the question, but I answered it and went back to my magazine. A few minutes later he asked me another question. I answered it and went back to reading.

The plane finally landed in Oakland, California. We walked into the terminal and exchanged pleasantries. He still had to wait about an hour for his flight to Hawaii. I headed for the exit. Before I got there he ran up to me: "Louis," he said, "if I become a Christian, does that mean I have to become a missionary or a preacher?"

"No," I said. "God needs laymen just as much."

———

THIS ALSO HAPPENED to me with the actress Susan Hayward. I was speaking at an Easter Sunrise Service at the Van Nuys Baptist Church, when we called for anyone who wanted to come forward to come forward. The actress Susan Hayward did.

Susan had been married to the actor Jess Barker, a friend of mine. They had fraternal twin boys. But that ten-year marriage was turbulent and ended in 1954. During that decade she'd been nominated for three best actress Oscars, and would get two other nominations—and win in 1959 for *I Want to Live*.

Apparently Susan wasn't happy. In April 1956 she tried to commit suicide with sleeping pills. I was driving up to the local mountains when I heard the news on the radio. She was in the old Cedars of Lebanon Hospital, on Fountain Avenue. I felt an urge to turn around and come home. I asked my wife, "Do you think I should try to see her?" and she said yes.

I drove back to Hollywood and parked near the Fountain Avenue Baptist Church. I knew the minister. I asked him to pray with me about my instinct to try to see Hayward. I didn't want to make a mistake. We concluded that I should.

The hospital lobby was jammed with reporters and cameras. She was listed under the name Mary Brennan, and no one was allowed to see Susan, not even the head of her studio, or her agent.

I got the receptionist's attention. "Can I help you?" she asked.

"Yes, I'm here to see Susan Hayward," I said, very softly.

"Well, so is everybody else."

"I know," I said, "Please call her room, and tell her it's Louis Zamperini. If she won't see me, I'll leave immediately."

The receptionist hesitated and was about to say no.

"But if you don't call her, I'm going to stay here all night," I added.

"Well, I'll call," she said, "but it won't do any good."

I appreciated that. She called. I got to go right up.

I slipped by the press and made for Susan's room. I knocked and walked in, expecting to see a depressed wreck. Instead, she looked great, lying in bed with the blanket pulled up to her chin.

"Well, hello, Louis," she said, cheerfully, then sat up.

We made a little small talk and then I got right to the point. "Why did you do this?" I asked. She didn't have a clear answer. The press later decided that she'd just been trying to get attention. But I took her seriously and said, "God has spared your life for a purpose." I wanted to let her know that the purpose was her salvation.

Susan's response caught me off guard: "Oh, well, I know that," she said. "God spared my life so I can make millions of people happy with my acting."

I didn't know what to say. We discussed what particular Bible verses meant, but every time I got close to discussing her walk down the church aisle, she deflected my question.

I wanted to press, but I'd done all I could.

"Don't feel too bad about my salvation," she said. "At least you taught me something—that I can ask God for whatever I need."

———

THE BIBLE SAYS to go into the world and preach the gospel, and some take this more seriously than others. But—and this has always been important to me—it doesn't say *anything* about forcing it down someone's throat. I can't say, "Hey, you've *got* to accept Him." And I don't.

Today, we have too many die-hard fundamentalists the world over. You can see the hate in their eyes when someone doesn't agree with everything they say. A dangerous few go to terrible lengths to spread their beliefs, including violence. I've met plenty of people who rejected Christ, yet it's always some guy trying to spread the word of one radical ideology or another who gets mad and madder because he believes he has to score a conversion, like it's a game he has to win.

If you go to the door and get rejected you're supposed to kick the dust off your shoes and move on, not try to kick down the door. You've done your job.

All you can do is plant the seed—whether it's about faith, some life lessons, or setting an example—and water it by answering any questions you're asked.

The rest isn't up to you.

# The Gangster and the Gospel

Jim Vaus was gangster Mickey Cohen's wiretapper. Like me, he became a Christian in November 1949, after listening to Billy Graham. There's a picture of me, Vaus, Stuart Hamblen (the singing cowboy), and Graham floating around out there.

Cohen was a juvenile delinquent, boxer, and gambler. He helped Bugsy Siegel set up the Flamingo Hotel in Las Vegas, and worked with him until Bugsy was murdered in 1947 when the mob became unhappy with his property management skills. Or so the story goes.

With Siegel gone, Cohen became the number-one mobster in Los Angeles, and as such was locked in a constant battle with Police Chief William Parker.

I knew Mickey Cohen. In those days, if you were a first-class athlete or a movie star, you'd meet guys like him all the time. But this relationship was more interesting than most.

———

There's a picture in *Devil at My Heels* of me meeting my wife-to-be at the Burbank airport just before we got married. Cynthia was the most beautiful girl in the world to me—and Mickey Cohen loved to meet athletes and pretty girls. I guess Cynthia and I satisfied all his requirements because Cohen told Jim Vaus, "I want to meet Zamperini." Recently converted, Vaus was happy to do it, hoping I might interest Cohen in a new way of life.

Cohen invited Cynthia and me to lunch. We met at the Brown Derby, the restaurant shaped like a hat, which by then had been physically moved from its original location up the street to 3377 Wilshire Boulevard. You walked around the rim to get in.

We had a nice conversation about our lives, USC football, my war story, and a little bit of Christianity. He wanted to know everything. He'd also say, "Pardon me," and get up about every ten minutes to use the bathroom. I thought maybe he had intestinal problems, but it was his hands. He was germ phobic.

Afterward, he'd sometimes ask us to lunch with him and whichever of his girlfriends were in town. Once he asked me to come to his haberdasher to meet a new girlfriend, a buxom blonde. This was Candy Barr, who became a famous stripper and burlesque dancer. She was sweet and friendly, but kind of naive. I guess he wanted us to know that he was more than a thug because he could have a nice girlfriend. Our meetings ended when he went to prison in 1951 for four years for tax evasion.

———

ONE NIGHT, AFTER he got out, Cohen called just as I was getting ready to go to bed. He told me where he lived and insisted I drive there immediately. As soon as my car touched the semicircular driveway automatic floodlights went on. Security guys escorted me to the front door. Inside, I could see he'd had a party. Half a turkey and a big ham were on the dining room table. Jim Vaus was there. Mickey offered me food, but it was past midnight.

He suggested we take a little tour. We stopped first at his closet. It had glass doors and was as long as a hallway inside. He must have had a hundred suits and pairs of shoes. And overcoats. "Anything that'll fit you, you can have," he said. I knew nothing would fit me. He was stocky and I was lean. I wouldn't have taken anything anyway. Jim Vaus was more his size. He got a beautiful overcoat.

Next, Cohen showed me his escape chute. In case of a raid, or if another gangster tried to kill him, he said he'd go down this chute. The door would automatically lock behind him and he'd end up in the basement.

"When I was in prison none of my friends visited me," he

said, with a sincere look. "Only Christians." He added that, as when we first met, he was still interested in Christ. I wasn't certain of his intent, and since the sun would be up in a few hours—and I had a meeting at noon—I told him we could talk about it anytime. I figured that if Cohen were serious I didn't have to rush it.

————

TWO WEEKS LATER, I was at the Coliseum for a football game, walking up the steps to get some food. John Ferraro, who was on the Police Commission, hollered at me: "Hey, Zamperini! What were you doing at Mickey Cohen's house a couple Saturdays ago?"

"You know what I was doing there!" I yelled back—meaning that I knew that he already knew. I could take a little ribbing.

To my surprise, Cohen got really gung ho on Christianity. He called me often. One day he announced, "I've been talking to the Sica brothers about Christ, but I don't have the knowledge. Will you go over there with me and tell them about Jesus?"

The Sica brothers were big Mafia. They were in the papers all the time and had every racket in town. But, I thought, why not?

Cohen and I went to a big flower shop on Vermont Avenue, near Olympic Boulevard. "Why are we stopping here?"

I asked. "Are you going to buy your girlfriend some more flowers?"

Instead, it was as if we were in a scene from an old gangster movie. We walked through the big cooler doors, found and opened another door, and ended up in a private room. There were the Sica brothers.

Cohen was thrilled to death, and I was excited that I'd get to discuss my faith with the Sica brothers.

When I explained, they said, "But we're Catholic."

"That's not the point," I said. "It makes no difference what you are."

Cohen had earlier told them my war story, and they seemed much more interested in hearing about that. Afterward, with a sidelong glance at Cohen, they thanked me for coming. I believe I bought some flowers for my wife on the way out.

———

MICKEY COHEN WAS desperate to meet Dr. Billy Graham. Even after all our talking, he said he wouldn't accept Christ as his savior unless it was directly through Graham.

Vaus and Hamblen wanted to make this happen. They were very eager and tended to act as the inspiration hit them, instead of thinking matters through. They arranged for a friend of ours from Modesto, who had a twin-engine Beechcraft, to fly down to Santa Monica airport to pick up Cohen and take him to Graham.

I had an odd feeling. "You're not going to make it," I said. "Why does he have to go to Billy Graham to find God? A ten-year-old kid can show anyone the way."

We were driving to Santa Monica to meet the plane, after an engagement at a church in Bakersfield. The whole way they tried to convince me that their plan was solid. "He's a criminal," I said. "He's been pulling the wool over everybody's eyes. He just wants the publicity that Billy Graham led him to the Lord."

They kept at me. I said, "I don't know what's going to happen, but you're not going to make it."

Of course, they didn't believe me. "The plane will be in Santa Monica in an hour and a half," Vaus said. "We've got Mickey ready to go, to fly him to Billy Graham."

We got to the airport and Cohen was waiting. Then we heard the Beechcraft. The pilot landed and headed for a line of planes parked on the ramp. Because the night watchman wouldn't turn on all the lights for one flight, the pilot didn't realize that there was a four-foot culvert between where he landed and where he wanted to park. By the time he realized it the plane was nose-down in the ditch. Tore up the motor.

I didn't say, "I told you so."

———

COHEN EVENTUALLY GOT his way, though. According to *Time* magazine in April 1957, after getting out of prison in 1955, Cohen, who said he was trying to go straight, met with Graham in Manhattan. Graham wasn't crazy about the publicity but he did say he'd gone to work on Mickey in 1949, "and I have high hopes that Cohen will repent in earnest."

Cohen's comment? "I am very high on the Christian way of life. Billy came up, and before we had food he said—what do you call it? That thing they say before food? Grace? Yeah, grace. Then we talked a lot about Christianity and stuff."

In June 1957, *Time* reported that "Graham . . . once said of [Cohen]: 'He has the makings of one of the greatest gospel preachers of all time.'"

Cohen never followed through. As far as I was concerned he just had the makings of a great con artist.

# Give Back

*Campers on their way to a new chance at life, 1955.*

# It Takes a Camp to Help a Child

When the head of the Fred C. Nelles School, a California State Youth Authority (CYA) facility in Whittier, asked me to talk to the residents (at the time we called them "wards of the state") I was eager to do it. (That school was later closed due to budget cuts. The CYA was renamed the Division of Juvenile Justice, and is part of the California Department of Corrections and Rehabilitation that provides education, training, and treatment services for California's most serious youth offenders.)

These were older kids, 16 to 20, in for all types of crimes, including homicide. But I didn't just want to show up and lecture. Lectures had never helped me when I got in trouble. I decided instead to share the story of how I'd been a first-class troublemaker who had once had the same poor attitude as my audience. I figured we could relate.

The kids seemed pretty impressed that I'd gotten away with so much. Then, I turned the tables. I explained how, with help and support, I'd transformed myself from a delinquent into an athlete. I finished with my prisoner-of-war experiences.

Let's just say they were surprised. They'd expected a sermon. Instead, I led them with me down Failure Road and then showed them that it was possible to get off that path and onto the Self-Respect Highway. I felt as if I were giving my younger self the support and advice, by example, that would have benefited me.

The next time I spoke to some CYA kids it happened again. And again. They seemed to finally realize that *they* had control over their own paths. I remember one group of boys who said, "Hey, after listening to your story, we can do our time standing on our heads."

Words are nice, but helping someone is all about action. I wondered: Did any of these boys have someone like my brother, Pete, in their lives? Did someone care enough not to give up on them? And if so, why hadn't it worked?

Maybe there was something more I could do to help.

———

SPEAKING TO THE boys at the Fred C. Nelles School led to an epiphany. I decided to help by creating the Victory Boys Camp in 1954. It was nonprofit and existed on donations. I set up the first camp on an abandoned campsite on the Angeles Crest Highway. The owner was a printer who belonged to my church. The accommodations were very basic but potentially wonderful: no electricity, but four cabins where I could house the kids, and another one I could use for a kitchen. There was also a freshwater stream, and water that came from an underground pump. The rent was cheap. We made a deal.

I signed on two other Olympians as counselors: Keith Wegeman and his older brother Paul. Keith was an Olympic ski jumper who competed in the 1952 Winter Games in Oslo, Norway. He later became a ski instructor and eventually moved to California to host a television series titled *Ski Tips* in the early 1960s. A couple of years later, we would scale the Gannett Glacier together.

Keith was also the body—but not the voice of—the Jolly Green Giant.

Paul, a Nordic combined skier, competed in the 1950 World Championships at Lake Placid, New York, and the 1952 Olympic Winter Games. He was also a big part of developing the Steamboat Springs recreation area in his home state of Colorado.

Most of the boys I met would explain their "crimes" as something they'd done "just for kicks." "I wanted a thrill." "For laughs!"

Athletics had changed my life, so my plan was to take about thirty-five troubled boys, mostly from the California Youth Authority schools and homes I had visited, for an

all-expenses-paid week of sports, survival skills, and an au-
thentic wilderness experience. In the evenings we'd sit around
the fire and talk about the day, about their lives. Sometimes
we'd talk about the Bible and I'd answer any questions, but
that was just one aspect of our program, and never forced.
All we asked for was respectful attention. If someone wanted
more information we were happy to answer questions afterward.

---

WE ONLY STAYED at the Angeles Crest Highway location for
a few years. During that time I was determined to improve
the camp and build a swimming pool.

Everyone told me construction was impossible because the
camp was at six thousand feet. "How will you get the water?
Even if you can, it will freeze in the winter. And there's no
power; you need two hundred and twenty volts to run the
filters."

You know me: I had to find a way.

I did need electricity. Because my speaking engagements
always generated goodwill, people who attended would
sometimes want to help. A construction company gave me
two Jeep motors. Each one was 110 volts. I put them in a
little shack, wired them together, and got the 220 volts I
needed to run pool filters—and more. They also gave me a
Jeep with a bulldozer blade. I could put the blade on or take

it off in less than two minutes. It came in handy clearing roads.

My biggest concern was finding a suitable spot for the pool above the local flood zone. A ranger showed me the highest water line from previous inundations, and we picked a site above any flood marks in memory. "If you put the pool here you'll be fine," he said. "Safe forever."

Great. But the plot was covered by a huge mound of dirt. To clear it I approached Elwain Steinkamp, who built Bel Air and belonged to my church. "I can help you," he said. "I'll bring up a D8 Caterpillar and three crews and their families. You provide a picnic for the women and the kids, and they'll remove that mound."

After the mound was gone I called a big pool building company. They inspected the ground and had bad news. "It's all gravel," they said. "We don't think it will hold together. But if by some miracle you can get the steel basket framework into the hole, and do the gunite, we'll do the rest for free."

I took that deal. Steinkamp dug the hole and, although it caved in here and there, I figured out a way to divert some of the freshwater stream into a moat around the hole, which made the walls slightly damp and more cohesive. The stream would also supply the water for the finished pool.

I worked with a crew to put in the rebar framework for a 22' by 45' pool. The gunite crew came next. Gunite is a mixture of cement, sand, and water that is pumped through a big hose and pneumatically sprayed at high velocity onto a mold—in this case, the steel framework. If you've watched a pool being built in your backyard, you know what I mean. A typical pool uses four inches of gunite over the steel basket. I needed gunite almost a foot deep to create a rigid structure.

When the pool company saw what we'd accomplished they kept their word, giving us stanchions and a springboard, a chrome ladder, a beautiful light for the bottom. I got the tile work done. I built a cabana at one end, and also put a seventeen-foot-wide cement deck and a four-foot wall around the deck. No way could a flood touch the pool. Everyone who saw what we'd accomplished couldn't believe it.

I filled the pool with water from the stream. Here's how: about 125 yards up the hill I built a small dam, with a two-inch nipple. I fused together 20-foot sections of black World War II rubber pipe, which is impervious to most everything, and ran it down the hill. Since the pipe was black and it ran above ground in the sun, the water arrived heated.

This may not seem like a big-deal story, but it shows what you can do when you put your mind to it.

———

AFTER THE POOL was in, my wife and I thought it might be great to own the property. The owner told us the price: $13,000. I didn't have the money. But that was okay. I had the camp, and the rent was reasonable.

So you can imagine that I wasn't pleased when the owner decided to triple the rent.

"What? I just built a pool."

"Yes, and now it's worth more. Sorry."

"But I've improved your property at my expense!"

He didn't budge. It didn't seem fair.

While I pondered what to do, unbeknownst to me the television host Ralph Edwards decided I should be a guest of honor on his extraordinarily popular show, *This Is Your Life*. No one told me, because that's how it worked: like a surprise party. The cover story was that the sportscaster Elmer Peterson wanted to interview me. I said sure. But when my driver got me to Peterson's studio, his door was locked. We went outside and stood next to these huge stage doors and waited.

"He'll be here any minute," the driver said.

Suddenly the stage doors opened and a bright light hit me in the face. I backpedaled. I heard a voice say, "Louis Zamperini" a few times. The driver walked me toward the light. There was Ralph Edwards. I'd handled crashing in an airplane, and being tortured in prison camp, but I was so astonished I couldn't move. "Louis Zamperini," Edwards said. *"THIS IS YOUR LIFE!"*

What I also didn't know is that the producers had asked my wife what great surprise gift they could get for me. She told them about the camp and the $13,000 price tag. But when they approached the owner, he suddenly wanted $25,000. Instead, the show gave me a beautiful gold wristwatch, a Bell & Howell movie camera, a thousand dollars in cash, and a 1954 Mercury Station Wagon.

I told the owner he could have the camp, the swimming pool, the flagpole, everything I'd built or improved—and made other plans.

———

YEARS LATER I ran into the campsite owner's daughter. "Are you still using the pool?" I asked.

"Oh no," she said. "A terrible flood blew it out of the ground."

"What?! That pool was made to be there forever."

She just shook her head. Seems there'd been a big fire on the mountain and the camp was gutted. Every single building on the property, every tree and shrub, burned to the ground. The place was useless. Then a heavy rain and flood did the rest. I was disappointed to learn that pool was lost, but I realized not being able to buy the camp had been a gift that had only revealed itself later.

Sometimes what we see as a loss turns out in the end to be a gain, and sometimes a gain is a loss. I try not to be too swift to pass judgment on any situation, preferring instead to be patient and take the long view because I believe that in the end all things work together for good.

# Get Their Attention

I had to move my camp to a different location, but had no idea where. So I went skiing at Mammoth Mountain and talked about my predicament with some friends. I met a woman and her husband who had a chalet. They said, "The summertime is slow, so bring your kids." Their place was like a first-class hotel. She also said, "I'm going to cook a lot of food and put it in the freezer so your kids will have food all summer." That was a big help.

The camp operated in both summer and winter. Now, instead of maintaining a permanent campsite, I could restructure the program and be more flexible. Dave McCoy, who ran Mammoth and was a lifelong friend, promised me free equipment and complimentary lift tickets for all the kids. As the years passed, we found different places to stay, like the old McGee Creek Lodge, where we got a great deal on room and board.

And the outdoors, of course, was free. I'd have the kids

climb on ice, ride horses in the High Sierras, cook outdoors, plunge into icy mountain streams—not to mention fish, swim, learn archery and how to handle firearms, camp in the wild, climb in the summer, and ski in the winter.

———

EVERY WEEK WE'D pick up a busload of new campers from one of the Youth Authority schools and drive north on Highway 395, on the east side of California. For most of the drive the boys would talk to each other and ignore me and Keith and Paul. Maybe they asked each other who we were, but they didn't have much to go on. They could also act surly and resentful. I understood. They knew in advance we'd come to rehabilitate them. They were frightened and unhappy and trying to look strong (particularly to each other), as if they didn't have a care in the world.

After a few hours we'd stop at Little Lakes, just off the road, southwest of Bishop. The area was covered in volcanic rocks and lava that had tiered because of water running through. I'd lead the group a mile into the hills to a dry waterfall called Fossil Falls. We'd climb to the top and I'd take them as close to the edge as was safe.

Some of the kids, full of a "Whaddaya trying to pull?" attitude, would always ask, "What are we gonna do here?"

I was about to show them. I secured my rope as best I could around a large rock, tied the other end around myself, and walked to the edge. I turned around to look at the group. I could see in their eyes that they thought I was crazy.

I jumped off the waterfall backward.

That got their attention.

The cliff was only thirty feet high but they were stunned because they couldn't see anything after I'd jumped. In fact, I was rappelling down the cliff face—and just getting started. I made my way back up and said, "Okay, fellows, every one of you is going to do that before we leave camp."

"Oh no, not me!"

"I can't do that."

"No way!"

I did it twice more. (And eventually so did each of them.)

Back on the bus the boys couldn't stop yakking or asking questions. Once they started talking to me, I had them. They'd gone from ignoring me to being on my side. Now I had their attention, which was the point.

It's tough to have a conversation if only one person is paying attention and the other individual has already made up their mind about what's what.

You need to break the stalemate by shifting their perspective. Thank goodness most of us don't have to jump off a cliff to do it.

# First You Listen

Keeping the boys active and involved was my primary focus, but it wasn't everything. I needed to get inside their heads and hearts. We had to talk to each other. I always told the boys that if they had any problems they could come to me or the camp counselors, Keith and Paul.

Somewhere inside each troubled young man, whether deep or near the surface, he wanted to open up to somebody who might actually listen. I saw it a thousand times: Getting the problem out in the open was a relief. It's hard to hold something monumental inside yourself without it turning into anger and fear and resentment. Talking helped the boys reveal their hearts and souls. It lightened the load.

I wanted to find out the nature of each boy's particular problem. Was he having trouble with his family? Stealing? Cutting classes? Fighting? Of course, you can't just start with "What's your problem?" You have to *really* listen. Listening is not a sign of weakness or of giving up your authority; it's a sign of strength. If you want to help you have to show a genuine interest, emphasis on genuine, and focus in. You can't fool kids, but they *will* talk if they trust you.

I made it my priority to be available at any time. I resisted being judgmental; that only creates opposition. I would never tell a boy that he was bad, or compare him to another boy and ask why he couldn't be more like him. That's not helpful. I might offer a little direction, but I never made decisions for my boys. The idea was to reach a point where *they* said, "Yeah, this is what I should do." Then I'd try to help them do it.

Often I started by using a topic I knew a lot about—as did most boys. Sports. I could talk about being an Olympian. If they liked football, I could talk about my time at USC. In fact, the coaches at USC were always helpful. I once worked with a broken family of five kids. To get their minds off the divorce, I took them down to the school. The football coach at the time, Ted Tollner, was thrilled. He said, "Louie, I'll do anything to help you. Every workout, the gate is closed to outsiders, but you're allowed to bring your kids in anytime, even before the UCLA game." After Ted, USC football coach Larry Smith was equally helpful. When those kids went on campus, met all those players, well, you can imagine, they became dyed-in-the-wool USC Trojans fans.

I also made a point of being versatile in other sports. If

they liked ice skating, I'd go ice skating. Or skateboarding. I could ski, climb, play tennis, cycle, and go rock climbing.

Once the boys began to open up, the process didn't stop with them realizing what to do that might help straighten out their lives. I couldn't just say, "Congratulations. You figured it out," and then drop them. That's like giving a person an aspirin to kill pain, when finding the cure for their pain is better. I had to make sure they didn't slack off. They needed a sense of direction. Goals. Just taking a bunch of kids to camp for a week is nice, but it's not enough.

# Accomplishment Is the Key to Self-Respect

Most "delinquents" (our term then) don't accomplish a darn thing. They don't finish what they start. They buy into the failure and feel sorry for themselves. They believe that's their lot in life.

I had to prove to them that they didn't have to be that way.

I geared every activity during the week around accomplishment. Depending on the season and location, I had something lined up every day: skiing, mountaineering, boating, archery, swimming, camping, using an ice axe, horsemanship, fishing, survival and rescue, first aid, and so on. I kept a chart with each boy's name on it, and each one would have to pass the requirements for every activity.

If one of the boys said, "I can't do it," we'd work with them until they got it. At the end of the week, I'd gather the kids and show them the chart and say, "You see what you've done this week? You've accomplished six different things.

You know they weren't easy." Sometimes they couldn't believe it themselves, which was fine. I wanted them to actually feel the pride and surprise of accomplishment and carry it with them when they left the camp. If it didn't sink in immediately, it would eventually.

I also sent the boys back with this message: "The main thing in life is to be able to accomplish something. You have one purpose now, and that's to serve your time, be good, get out of that place, and go back and finish your high school education." (They could finish it in the schools, too, since the California Youth Authority/Department of Juvenile Justice was legally required to provide a full high school education.)

I always had a few boys who would say something like, "I've always been a dummy and I can't get a degree."

"If you want a degree, then go for it," I'd say. "But you can make good money without a degree." A degree is preferable, but not having one shouldn't prevent anyone from doing what truly interests them.

To help the boys focus on possible futures, I made a series of vocational films. They were geared to the times: working with sheet metal, plating, creating antique glass, and other trades. Now it would be all about computers, I'm sure.

As I told interviewer George Hodak in 1988 when we spoke for the LA84 Foundation, "Today, in this world of competition, high finances, high salaries, and big money in sports, I'd say that you have to be an actual expert in more than one field in case you need to change directions due to circumstances beyond your control, like the economy, or because your heart tells you to follow your passion. Just don't be afraid to make mistakes; they are just the stepping-stones to success."

# My Private Reward

One great reward of running Victory Boys Camp was quite unexpected. I'd be speaking at a church or on a cruise ship when a middle-aged guy would stand up and say, "I was in your camp when I was fourteen. You really turned my life around."

They did the turning; I only tried to show the way. I still felt great.

A few years ago I spoke to about 250 men at a business club. Afterward an older man approached and shook my hand.

"Louis," he said, "you probably wouldn't remember me. My name is . . ."

When he told me, I said, "Stop. You were from Glendale."

"How could you remember?"

"After what you did? How could I forget?"

The kid's neighbors had gone to Europe. He and his buddies went to the beach and picked up a couple of girls. One of them had a bottle of whiskey, so they got drunk. They held the party in the neighbors' house after breaking in. They ate the neighbors' food, used their pool, and shacked up on the veranda above the garage. Then, when the girls left, the boys took furniture from the house and threw it into the pool. Stinkers!

Tough to forget.

He came to my attention when one of the service clubs, the Optimists or the Rotary, called me and said, "This kid's in real serious trouble." I took him to camp and straightened him out. Eventually he became the president of an insurance company. Insurance? After he'd caused his neighbors to use theirs? I thought that was pretty funny.

Some men are afraid to say they were at my camp. They're worried about their reputations. They shouldn't be. They made it out. They did well. For me, there's no greater reward than seeing once frightened and unhappy boys change into strong citizens who lead positive lives.

# The Mission That Never Ends

It seems that the older I get the more I'm involved with young people. It's the thrill of a lifetime. One reason is that my books have spread the word and I keep getting letters like this one: "I'm like you, I'm in trouble all the time, but the book has changed me."

I love hearing from kids who were on the wrong track.

The actual, physical camp is closed, but I didn't end its mission, which will continue even after I'm gone. In fact, I'm willing to help any kid that's in trouble, to get him out of his mess, and to get him under an inspirational and stiff disciplinary program. So many kids can be helped, and that's why even though I couldn't participate in person at the camp anymore—no more mountaineering—I didn't abandon the program.

I just sent a young man named Kyle to a special school in Australia. It's the cream of the crop. He knew my son, Luke, and his wife, Lisa. Kyle was caught in a whirlwind of drugs, but said he was fed up with his life. I paid his way, I paid for the camp. The people who run the place told me they just couldn't believe how wonderfully he'd changed for the better.

Doing something like that is worth every penny.

## KYLE GAUTHIER

*When you stop and think about the people you most respect in this world, those you truly admire and look up to, whose words match the truth of their hearts—you realize that you've probably known these people for years, maybe even a lifetime. It takes time to build something like that.*

*At present, I've known the name Louis Zamperini for about six months. I met him a single time. And yet I can tell you with all of my heart that I truly love and respect this man.*

*Six months ago I was about to walk into a beautiful house in the Hollywood Hills, the kind of house that I'd only seen in movies. I was a lost, scared boy who at the time had no sense of hope or direction. Even more daunting, I was curious why a rich, old man whom I'd never met wanted to give a lying, cheating junkie like myself thousands of dollars.*

*See, in my life then I was the kind of guy who would steal your wallet and then help you look for it. Few people trusted me. I wanted to change, and I'd been accepted to a school in Australia, a Christian organization called Youth With A Mission. But I was broke and this guy didn't know about the six other failed attempts of sending me away to get better.*

*So I was all ears when this offer came along.*

*The first things I saw in the house were Olympic torches, flags, and pictures of him and famous people. I saw sports gear and WWII gear and felt like I had walked into a museum. I thought, Who the hell is this guy!? He must be hardcore.*

*That meant I had to step up my game.*

*I put on the most sober, well-put-together, professional face I could and prepared myself for the interrogation I was certain would come. I framed answers in my head (lies) to the expected questions like, "How motivated are you?" "How long have you been clean?" "What are your plans?"*

*Louis's daughter-in-law, Lisa, was with me. "Louie, this is Kyle," she said. "The one going to Australia."*

*Louis looked up at me. "Huh? Australia? I love the shopping in Australia."*

*My mouth gaped. I sat down as he continued to talk—literally for hours, telling me story after story of sailing through in the Pacific Ocean, of running track, of the strategies he and his gang would use, when he was young, to steal the best pies they could from the local baker. I felt as if I was listening to a kids' adventure book about the life you dream of living as a child.*

*But I noticed something even more amazing than the stories—and his life in general: it was the absolute humble heart in every word Louis spoke. It was as if no one that*

Louis knew, and nothing that had happened in his astounding life, really impressed him as much as they impressed others. He was impressed by something even greater.

I remember looking at a picture of Louis and USC football coach Pete Carroll on the desk. I've always been a huge USC fan. I said, "Louis, you know Pete Carroll?!"

"Oh, yeah," he said, casually. "He keeps calling. He wants me to speak to his team or something."

He was so nonchalant that I thought that either his age had addled him—Louis was about to turn 97—or there was something wildly special about him, something that I had never encountered in anyone else.

When I finally left Louis's house, I was more confused than when I'd arrived. Not once did he mention the money he was giving me. Not once did he ask any of the questions I'd created ready answers for. For some reason he was willing to trust me. I didn't know why. My plan walking in was to go to Australia as an escape, a way to get clean, to clear my head, and maybe meet a girl—or two. After meeting Louis that plan changed in a way that I couldn't yet understand. He didn't just leave me with money. He gave me something bigger through a glimpse of his heart. Now I had to discover what it was.

The school in Australia was the hardest thing I'd ever done in my life. I was challenged in ways I didn't know existed. At times I wasn't sure I'd make it; sometimes I didn't want to *make it. It seemed easier to quit. I wasn't afraid of failing. I'd been living with myself for so long, attempting to get better in my own ways, and so often failing, that I was used to it. Now, I was scared of succeeding. I was scared to actually let all the grace and blessings I'd been given change me.*

*The fear only got worse as I stood before hundreds of people on the beach of Byron Bay, a city with a high incidence of drug abuse, because now I had to make a choice and declare it in front of everyone. Fail or succeed? I knew what I desperately wanted.*

*The moment they raised me from the baptizing waters, the fear was gone. I could finally see for myself the "something" greater, bigger, and special that I had seen in Louis. It was clear why nothing in this world could compare to what was in his heart—because it couldn't.*

*No story, no fame, no amount of money, no drug, no drink, no woman can ever compare to the truth and love that Louis knew and helped reveal to me: of having a true, real relationship with Jesus Christ.*

*When Louis died all I could do was ask, "God, how can I repay this man, thank this man that was so obedient to you and helped change my life?"*

*The answer became clear: I would devote my entire life to doing the same work Louis did and let God use me to help the lost people of this world, and to love people when they seemingly don't deserve to be loved—like Louis did for me.*

# What I've Learned

*Louis airborne, 1983, challenging himself as always.*

# Challenge Yourself

In August 1957, Olympian Keith Wegeman and I decided to climb to the top of Gannett Glacier in Wyoming, and make an inspirational film to show at the Victory Boys Camp. Gannett was the largest perennial ice and snow field in the Rocky Mountains of North America. It rests on the east and north slopes of Gannett Peak, which at 13,809 feet is the highest mountain in Wyoming, in the Wind River Range.

Gannett Glacier is about 110 miles south of the Grand Tetons, but neither Keith nor I had ever been there. Both of us were pilots, though, so we rented an airplane and overflew the vicinity to pinpoint our destination. We had a picture to help us.

Afterward, we took the plane back, gathered up all the equipment we needed, including our skis and a movie camera, and drove to Dubois, Wyoming—the closest town. The ranger, who was also the sheriff, gave us some general directions to the glacier; since there was no easy access or modern trail then, we had to find our own way in. A farmer rented us a horse and a mule, and we hiked to Fish Hatchery Road, where we picked up the trail. The glacier base was about fifty miles into the wilderness area, and that meant elk, moose, and bear country.

Keith's brother, Paul, had planned to come with us, but backed out at the last minute. Instead, my wife, Cynthia, came. I had misgivings, but she insisted. "You're not the only adventurous person in this family," she insisted, and she was right. For our honeymoon, I had suggested going either to Hawaii or to a war buddy's cabin near the Eel River, south of Eureka, California. Cynthia chose the mountains. As a Miami native, whose family had money and had sent her to the finest schools, she knew enough about lying around on the beach. "Let's do the other," she said. We had a great time. We swam, rode horses, fished. Cynthia got to be a crack shot with the .22. When she almost stepped on a rattlesnake she whipped out the pistol and plugged it in the head.

It took us a couple of days to get to the glacier. The only people we met on the way were a couple of sheepherders. We camped the first night at Ink Wells, the name of which refers to a trio of lakes, all pitch-black, and whose depth had never been measured.

The next day we reached the Wind River Wilderness area. The Wind River is fed from the Gannett Glacier. We crossed the river and then went up about five miles toward the glacier, and found the camp area and a huge, sturdy teepee. We believed it belonged to the legendary Chief Washakie, who had been the head of the Eastern Shoshones, and lived to 102.

We set up base camp and built a big fire pit with small boulders. To stay warm as night settled in we used a trick I knew. Boulders don't get burning hot, they just get warm. So you take one, wrap a towel around it, and put it in your sleeping bag. You'll sleep like a baby.

———

WE HAD FIGURED it would take all day to climb to the top of the glacier, but we got a late start. Rather than wait another day, when the weather might not be good, Keith and I decided that to make the top we'd just have to move a little more quickly than planned. That meant leaving behind some of the climbing gear. Should we take the rope and crampons, or the ice axe? It seemed we'd use the ice axe more. Also, we were Olympians, and in top shape. We figured we could actually climb it in half a day.

We set out under sunny skies, wearing khakis and army boots. But just to be on the safe side, I told my wife, "If we're not back by dark, there's something wrong. Saddle the horse, ride out, and get help."

Keith and I started up. I shot some footage and we made great progress. The skies stayed clear—and then out of nowhere a storm hit. Suddenly we had snow and lightning. In order to avoid being struck, we had to toss our metal ice axes a safe distance away. It was tough to hold them anyway, since our fingers were starting to cramp and freeze in the wind. We needed to find a windbreak and luckily noticed an indentation in the ice. We fashioned a little cave that we could fit into and wait it out.

"I think we made a mistake trying to climb the north face," Keith said. He was right. The snow there was always fluffy and dangerous. On the south face the sun hit the snow. It would melt and then harden again overnight, creating an icepack. Very sturdy. But on the north face you could step in the wrong place and kill yourself by falling into a crevasse that you never knew was underfoot.

The storm was short-lived, but it was growing colder. We sat in our cave trying to decide whether to keep going or turn back.

We went on. No storm now, just low-hanging cloud cover. It wasn't much farther to the top, and just as we got there the sky lifted. In the panoramic window between the cloud bottoms and the horizon we could see the mountains in every direction. It occurred to me then that the whole climb had been a metaphor: We suffered, we struggled. It was brutally cold and painful. It was just like life, and the reward was this glorious sight. A heaven on earth.

This beautiful vision was sadly temporary. The sun began

to sink quickly and that killed our reverie. We'd taken half a day to get to the top of the glacier, we'd been transfixed by the vista, and now it would be dark in thirty minutes. You don't want to be 13,000 feet up on a glacier at night. We had to get down in a hurry.

Fortunately, Keith and I were both competent boot skiers and glissaders. And luckily we'd made the right decision to take the ice axes. (Of course, we should also have brought the rope. Never climb without a rope!) You hold the ice axe's T-handle and put the sharp end in the snow. Then you literally ski on your boots. To increase speed you lean forward. To slow down, pull back on the axe. The north side was too risky because of the hidden crevices, so we went straight down the icy south slope. We needed less than thirty minutes to get down, at speeds of almost thirty miles an hour. I can't say we enjoyed the glide. There's nothing like an icy wind to ruin your day when you're not dressed for it.

By the time we were down it was pitch-dark. We found the gear we'd left at the bottom lip of the glacier. And the mule. We put on warm jackets and dug out some matches. We tied ourselves together with a rope and lit match after match trying to avoid falling into the stream while working our way back to my wife.

Eventually we saw a blaze. Cynthia had started the fire. But instead of saddling the horse and riding out to get help, she sat there crying. I fired a pistol I'd packed into the air, to let her know we were nearby. When she finally saw us, she came running up. I was glad she'd stuck around.

Keith and I had been overconfident—okay, idiots—to believe we could race the day to the top, with half our equipment, and get down in daylight. We'd been arrogant. At least we'd both had survival training, and knew how to use our equipment.

That kept us from being dead idiots.

That said, I'm glad we made the climb. No matter how old you are, don't stop challenging yourself with new experiences, but be smart about it, please.

# Learn to Adapt

Under the Older Americans Act of 1973, my church was designated as a proposed site for a nutritional program for seniors. I interviewed with the city of Los Angeles to run it, and before I got back home they had called. My wife said, "You got the job."

I was already working with young people through my camp, and speaking to schools. Now, working with the elderly, I had to get up to speed and learn about nutrition. I had to create the proper atmosphere at the lunch program to reduce loneliness. I had to help find housing. I got close to the seniors, and as must happen in life, some of them died.

The death of someone you know takes a lot out of you, and even though death was familiar to me from the war, I had to learn to cope with it all over again. I took classes at USC, read books on stress and burnout, and discovered that burnout is at least in part a response to chronic unreleased stress. One way to deal with stress is to stay as active as you can, and burn off the burnout.

When George Hodak interviewed me for the LA84 Foundation, he asked if my athletic and war injuries—and, frankly, my age—had limited my ability to ski or skateboard or otherwise stay active. This is what I told him:

*You have to learn to adapt. You can't give up. My bad knee is painful, and a bad ankle and back as well—and the pain is always there. But what am I supposed to do? Pull in my wings and be grounded? You have to use unrelenting determination and exercise a positive attitude. I had to learn to ski with a certain style that eliminated the pressure on my knee. I found that going down the steepest runs at Mammoth is less painful than skiing on the bunny slopes below. So I prefer to ski the hazardous slopes. And then, of course, I skateboard every day to keep myself tuned up and sharpened. I think my skateboarding shakes up a few people, especially some of the old-timers in the church. When I go down the street and make a run to the mailbox I've seen people stop their cars and look back to be sure their eyes aren't deceiving them. They see this gray-haired old buzzard weaving down the street. (Laughter.) I guess it is kind of a shock to them. It doesn't bother me. I just think of myself as a kid. I treat myself as a youngster. I ignore the aches and the pains. I have to.*

It's like I always say: You can't just talk about how you live your life. You have to live it.

I know it works, as this letter I got a few years ago demonstrates. (I save them all and wish I still had time to answer every one as well.)

"*My experiences during my formative years initially led me to believe that the measure of a man is based on the size of his paycheck or his house or how many goals he can accomplish at the expense of others. I now know that the measure of a man is based on how he lives his life each day, and what he contributes rather than takes from society. Thank you, Mr. Zamperini.*"

I think that says it all.

# Commitment and Perseverance Pay Off

People often ask me what I've learned in life that is worth remembering and passing on. Here's something I say, especially to young people: It will be tough to amount to anything unless you commit to your goal and stay the course. You can't give in to doubt. You can't give in to pain.

Becoming a great athlete, writer, businessman, whatever, doesn't just happen. You have to reach deep within yourself to discover if you're willing to make the necessary sacrifices. If not, choose another goal, and ask the question again.

This is the great lesson of my life: Never give up. If you want to be a champion you have to go after what you want tooth and nail. This requires perseverance. If you're on the right track, stay on that path until you've finished.

Take athletes: Many are very good, and some even reach the threshold of greatness, but only the athlete who is disciplined, who uses continual self-analysis for improvement of both the physical and mental aspect of his or her being, will ever have a chance to take a step beyond that threshold and taste excellence and glory.

Even if you don't end up as the greatest at what you do, as long as you do your best you should be satisfied. After all, there are only so many places on the Olympic team. There is only one boxing champion at a time. A corporation has one CEO. The country has one president. Getting to the top takes natural talent and luck as well as hard work. That shouldn't discourage you from aspiring. You can't control the first two, but you are in charge of the last—which puts you in a position to discover if you have natural talent, and see what luck brings. Don't shortchange yourself in the effort department, no matter how tough it is. We can't all be champions, but we can give whatever is in us to give.

My older brother, Pete, put it all in sharp perspective for me when I was young and trying to become a championship runner: "Isn't one minute of pain worth a lifetime of glory?"

# You're Only as Old as You Feel

My college years at USC were about more than running. I also liked to have a good time. What college student doesn't?

In those days, when society people took a vacation they called the newspaper, which printed their plans. *"Mr. and Mrs. Edward Talbott are going to the West Indies for two weeks, from January 17 to February 2."* Today we wouldn't dream of making that information public. There'd be so many criminals in front of the house they'd have to draw straws to see who got to rob it first.

Weddings were also announced ahead of time in the paper. Harry Read and I saw that as an opportunity to have some fun. Our idea: Two smart and adventurous young men could show up, get lost in the crowd, and eat and drink for free. And meet girls. We were wedding crashers.

We tried it first at a wedding at the Knickerbocker Hotel. We wore black suits and white shirts and slicked back our hair. We lingered near the entrance and eavesdropped to pick up any information we could. Then when a car pulled up and everyone got out, we'd shake the new arrivals' hands like we were with the wedding party—perhaps mentioning a name or two—and walked in with the group.

Once inside, we could have made a beeline for the buffet, or scouted out the young ladies. Instead we found the older women, the aunts and grandmothers to whom no one paid much attention—especially if they didn't look like they were having a great time. We admired their jewelry and their dresses, brought them food and drinks, talked, and had a dance or two before moving on to chasing the younger gals. We sincerely enjoyed ourselves, and had some unexpectedly interesting conversations.

We also figured that if someone wanted to toss us out, our new friends might vouch for us as well-behaved and harmless. If that didn't happen, we would, of course, just tell the truth—slightly embellished. "We're athletes from USC and we read about the wedding and just couldn't resist attending."

Unrestrained enthusiasm worked wonders, especially if we dressed well.

We crashed eight weddings.

Now, I'm 97, and about thirty years ago I finally understood that our "transactions" with the aunts and grandmothers was actually a two-way street—only they didn't let on and we weren't smart enough to realize it. They knew exactly what we were up to and enjoyed every minute of our doting attention. They were way ahead of us in years, as well as in wisdom.

Now that I'm a senior citizen, I love it when young people pay attention to me. Plus, I get to find out what the young people are up to—which keeps me young. And I might just be able to pass along something that will come in handy for them as time goes by.

I sure hope so.

# Free Advice

1. When I get on an airplane, before I even sit down, I look around for the exit doors. When the flight attendant does the safety demonstration, I already know where I'm going.

   Awareness equals survival.

   When I walk down the street I can spot guys, from half a block away, that could harm me. I cross over. If they cross, too, then I head for a store or wherever there are people. Once, I saw two kids coming down Hollywood Boulevard, their eyes fixed on me. They figured the old man's got money in his pocket. A woman in front of me was pulling a basket with groceries in it. I leaped over the basket. When they saw me leap, they realized I wasn't an easy mark. They turned and went the other way.

   Awareness saves your life.

   I credit physiology classes I took from Dr. Roberts at

USC with making me aware of the importance of always being aware. As I told the *USC Family* magazine in 2003, *"I tell kids to be aware of what's going on around them, in the street, in class, to size up the situation, think of the consequences. It's the one thing schools neglect to teach in the classrooms, and it's the answer to all the choices we make and to all survival in this world.*

*"Dr. Roberts (my physiology professor) called it mind-over-matter. But you could also call it wisdom."*

2. I once walked into a bank and saw a big burly guy and his girlfriend. They weren't standing in line. They had fistfuls of money, and panic on their faces. And a gun. He came at me as I opened the door. He put the gun in my face and said, "Step aside!" A few bills fell to the floor from the girl's hand. She stooped to pick them up.

"Yes, sir," I said, and did what he asked. They ran out.

For a moment, the bank was so quiet you could have heard those bills drop. I scanned the room. Those who had watched the holdup stood there, eyes glazed. Suddenly, one man ran toward the door behind me. "Oh, oh, oh . . . I'm getting outta here!" he yelled as he pushed through. Like sheep, everyone followed him. Why? The bank was safe now, but who knew what was happening on the street? The police were probably on their way, and the guy had a gun.

I would have had a twenty-minute wait to make a deposit, but I just walked up to a teller and was first in line.

We've all read stories about someone who, faced with a gun or some other weapon, argues.

"Give me your wallet!"

"But . . ."

Or they try to be a hero.

I remember a famous attorney—they called him a fighter—who came out of a nightclub in Hollywood and got robbed in the parking lot. Being an attorney, he tried to reason with the thief. He didn't use his much-praised head, and got shot and killed instead. People said, "Well, he got shot because he was a fighter; he fights back at anything."

Well, no more. If a guy's got a gun, and you're not on the battlefield, humble yourself.

3. I married Cynthia Applewhite—the girl of my dreams—in 1946. She died in 2001. We had fifty-five years together, raised two great kids, had a wonderful grandson and a terrific son- and daughter-in-law. Cynthia and I also let each other lead our own lives. You know what I did, which took me away from home

much of the time. Cynthia was an artist, a published novelist, an adventurer who once traveled around the world for three months on tramp steamers. She was always coming up with something.

When I worked at my local church, because of my reputation I would occasionally be asked for advice and counsel on how to keep a marriage together. It's a great responsibility, and a rough game. When times are tough you have to keep the parties from jumping on each other.

Here's what I did: I talked to the husband and wife separately. I'd tell each of them something my brother Pete once told me. "When you're wrong, admit it. When you're right, keep your mouth shut." I'd also tell the husband: "Whatever you do, do not tell your wife what I just told you." To the wife, I'd say: "This is the secret to a happy marriage but under no circumstance tell your husband what I just told you."

Many of those couples stayed together a long time.

# Lessons of the
# Olympic Spirit

*At seventy-nine, carrying the torch through Playa del Rey,
California, for the 1996 Summer Olympics
in Atlanta, Georgia.*

# It's About People

The Olympic Spirit is not about winning. It's not about gold medals.

It's about people.

When I came home after the 1936 Olympics, I wrote down what I thought about my experience. Then I put it in a drawer. Forty-eight years later, when I was asked to run with the torch for the 1984 Olympics in Los Angeles, I dug it out, rewrote it, and showed it to the Olympic Committee:

*"The Olympic Spirit is like the wind. You don't see it coming or going but you hear its voice. You feel the power of its presence. You enjoy the results of its passing. And then it becomes a memory, an echo of days of glory."*

To my surprise they asked to use it. Not bad for a nineteen-year-old kid. I'm glad I saved it.

# You Have to Train
# to Carry a Torch

————

You've done your best in training. You've made the Olympic team. That's the goal: *make the team*. You can't put the
euphoria into words. You discover a world beyond the competition, meeting foreign athletes who have had the same
thrilling experience. The camaraderie binds you.

When the Games end you want to do it again.

Most of us don't get to go back, unless we are honored by
being asked to be part of the worldwide Olympic torch relay.

Running with the torch is among my most cherished
memories. I ran five times: Los Angeles/1984, Atlanta/1996,
Nagano/1998, Sydney/2000, and Salt Lake City/2002. That's
a record.

The flame symbolizes the theft of fire from Zeus, by Pro-
metheus, which he then gave to man. The modern-day torch
relay started in 1936, ending at the Berlin Olympics, in which
I competed. The flame was lit by the sun reflecting off a con-

cave mirror in Olympia, Greece, and transported over 3,187 kilometers by 3,331 runners in twelve days and eleven nights from Greece to Berlin. (In the movie version of *Unbroken*, my grandson, Clay, plays the final relay runner who lights the Olympic flame in the stadium.)

When I was asked to run in Los Angeles in 1984, my whole family was excited. My daughter, Cissy, even wore shorts and running shoes to the event and ran as close to me as the police escort would allow. She kept saying, "That's my dad," to everyone in the crowd that lined the street.

For the 1998 Winter Olympics, Cissy flew with me to Japan to once again run beside me and cheer me on just out of camera range. I carried the torch in Joetsu, near where I had been imprisoned more than fifty years earlier.

There's no other feeling like running with an Olympic torch. You stand there looking for the approaching runner. Where is he? Where is she? Eventually a speck appears down the road and grows larger and larger as it approaches. And then it's your turn. Every runner has their own torch, lit by the previous runner, and then you light the next. The flame is transferred and you're off.

You have to carry the torch one kilometer—about three-quarters of a mile—in less than nine minutes. In 1984, I was sixty-seven years old. I wanted to be in the best shape, so I ran two kilometers a day to train and got my time down to 3:50.

I was supposed to run alongside Zamperini Field in

Torrance (the airport was renamed after me as Zamperini Memorial Field—but when I came home they dropped the Memorial), because it went right down Pacific Coast Highway a half block from the airfield. But the officials made a mistake and got the airfield wrong. I ran at LAX instead.

When I finished my leg, I lit the torch of Mack Robinson's son—without knowing it. Mack Robinson was a silver medalist in the men's 200 meters at the 1936 games. Jesse Owens only beat him by a foot and .4 seconds. Baseball great Jackie Robinson was Mack's younger brother.

Eventually, the torch arrived at the Olympic Stadium as part of the opening ceremony. At the 1936 Games in Berlin, as part of the spectacle, they released thousands of pigeons into the air to symbolize doves, which stood for peace. Our team stood on the field wearing Buster Keaton straw hats. Lucky break. The pigeons flew. And circled. And dropped on everyone. We were supposed to stand at attention, but it was hard not to laugh.

Little-known fact: The birds used to be released *before* the lighting ceremony, but because some of the birds would settle down on the edge of the cauldron, unfortunate accidents occurred. Now they light the flame first, and the birds know enough to stay far away.

Of all my torches, the LA torch was the only one that you could actually light at any time. The handle was a propane container. You lit the top felt with lighter fluid, then opened the propane to make the flame bigger. Subsequent torches didn't work that way. When the juice ran out that was it.

I took the LA torch to lots of schools. I'd stand onstage and light it, and the kids could come up and have their pictures taken.

In Japan for the 1998 Nagano Winter Olympics, I started running in Joetsu—once called Naoetsu. The flame had arrived the night before and was kept on hold for the ceremony. There was a banquet. In the morning we went to a tent. Introductions were made and little speeches given. The mayor said, "Welcome to Joetsu under different circumstances." Then I took my torch, held it high, and the previous torchbearer lit it. I turned to the crowd so that they could see—and I started to run.

I wore a beautiful light running suit, but I'd trained in my regular clothes plus a couple of extra sweaters for the cold—as well as to add extra weight. Most people don't realize that you have to train to carry a torch. They're not terribly heavy—maybe four pounds—but you have to hold it up high the whole way. And smile. And wave. Your arm muscles need to be fit.

I've met torch carriers who forgot (or never knew) this; then their arm starts killing them and slowly drops down. They're miserable. But they don't have to be. Guess what? You can switch hands. It's okay. People will think you just want to wave to the crowd on the other side of the road.

As long as you've prepared and do your best, there's no shame in being flexible.

# Forgiveness Is the Healing Factor

*Louie truly became a different person, able to forget the bitterness and sincerely forgive.*

—Cynthia Applewhite Zamperini, 1999

Over the many years since World War II I've thought about what happened to me in Japan, and about the Bird specifically. Just to check myself now and then I'd think of the Bird getting off scot-free and wait to see how I felt. Nothing. It didn't bother me a bit.

A man at Universal Pictures once said to me, "You've forgiven the Japanese, but don't you condemn them for what they did?" I thought about it: True forgiveness goes hand in hand with no longer condemning. Some people forgive and then keep thinking, "That son of a gun, what he did to me." But is that forgiveness? When you forgive you have to let it go.

———

IN LATE 1997, when CBS producer Draggan Mihailovich was putting together *The Great Zamperini*, a thirty-five-minute feature on me for the 1998 Winter Olympics at Nagano, he called one day and said, "Get a hold of your chair."

"Okay, I got a hold of my chair," I said. "What's up?"

"I found the Bird. He's alive."

"What!" When I'd gone back to Japan in 1950, I visited Sugamo prison, where the men who had imprisoned me were then incarcerated. I wanted to see them face-to-face, to look into their eyes and offer forgiveness. I had hoped to see the Bird there, but he'd disappeared and everyone thought he'd committed suicide. What really happened is that Mutsuhiro Watanabe had hidden in a mountain cabin in the hills of Nagano for years, returning only after the general amnesty.

"Yeah, we found him. We're going to have to corner him and get an interview. Would you like to see him?" Draggan asked.

"Absolutely," I said.

Draggan had tracked down the Bird, called his home, and spoken to his wife. He asked if an interview was possible. She said he was sick. A couple of days later, Draggan called again. This time Watanabe's wife said, "He's on a trip."

Draggan and his crew, including veteran CBS reporter Bob Simon, who reported the story, decided to hide and watch the house. They discovered that Watanabe took long walks, so they set up a camera across the street, and hid a small camera in a crew member's hat. When the Bird came out, they approached him and speaking through a translator asked if he was Watanabe.

"Yes, I'm Mutsuhiro Watanabe," he said. After the usual formalities he agreed to speak.

When asked if he knew Louis Zamperini, the Bird said, "Ah, Zamperini-ka. Orympi-ka. Number-one prisoner. I remember him well. Good prisoner."

"Would you like to see him?"

To my surprise, the Bird had said, "Yes."

In the middle of the interview, Watanabe's son and grandson came out of the house and discovered what was going on. As they listened they heard Bob Simon say, "Well, if [Zamperini] was such a good prisoner, why did you beat the hell out of him?"

Watanabe spoke very little English, but he understood. "He said that?"

"Zamperini and the other prisoners remember you in particular as being the most brutal of all the guards," Simon asked. "How do you explain that?"

"Beating and kicking in Caucasian society are considered cruel behavior," the Bird explained. But there were some occasions, he suggested, in which beating and kicking were unavoidable. "I wasn't given military orders," the Bird explained, "but because of my own personal feelings . . . I treated the prisoners strictly as enemies of Japan. Zamperini was well-known to me. If he says he was beaten by Watanabe, then such a thing probably occurred at the camp."

Watanabe's family was shocked. They didn't know his history. They were upset by the old man trying to find the correct words. They stopped the interview, and told the crew to leave and not come back.

I can't blame them for that. Any son, no matter whether his father is right or wrong, is going to back his father.

Draggan stopped filming, but asked Watanabe if he still wanted to meet with me. Again, he said yes.

Draggan tried to arrange a get-together but the son adamantly refused. "Mr. Zamperini will expect my father to bow and scrape and ask forgiveness."

When Draggan told me that I said, "No. I'm not going to ask him to ask for forgiveness. I've already forgiven him."

Efforts to get us together continued. I wrote a letter to the Bird and carried it to Japan. In it, I told him about my conversion and how it had led to forgiveness. But the Bird still did not want to meet, and that was that. I gave the letter to someone who said he could get it to Watanabe. I don't know if it ever arrived.

In 2003 Watanabe died.

Of course, I've thought often about what I might have said or done had we been able to meet. I imagined introducing myself, chatting, suggesting lunch. I'd ask about his family. If the war came up I'd say it was unfortunate that we'd even had a war. Otherwise, I wouldn't speak of it, or accuse him of crimes. The one who forgives never brings up the past to that person's face. When you forgive, it's like it never happened.

True forgiveness is complete and total. Of all the wonderful results of changing my life, perhaps the best is my ability to forgive.

———

BEFORE RETURNING TO Japan for the Winter Olympics, I asked Draggan Mihailovich if he could work it out so that I could run with the torch alongside my prison camp.

Draggan said that CBS had to go to the Japanese Olympic Committee, Coca-Cola, and our Olympic Committee to get permission for me just to carry the torch. He also got together with the people who had established the Peace Park in Joetsu, and went to the mayor. Originally, the Japanese only wanted Japanese in the relay on their home soil. But they agreed, and I was the only outsider.

The whole idea of a dedicated Peace Park is phenomenal. Of all the former POW camp sites, only Joetsu did this. When they realized the truth of what had happened in their city, they didn't want anyone to forget: not themselves, their kids, or their kids' kids. They pitched in, pooled their resources, bought the land, and created the Peace Park. "It's beautiful that you've forgiven all that happened here," the mayor told me, "but we should never forget."

Carrying the torch through the town where I was a prisoner of war was both thrilling and touching. Our minds have movies that play and replay, and I couldn't stop picturing the camp. We were slave labor. I was beaten almost on a daily basis. I had hated the people. I thought about all my buddies dying. I had fantasized about getting revenge.

And then there I was running with thousands of cheering people lining the road, many of them school kids. They received me with love and graciousness. I felt like a king.

To tell you the truth, although I'd made my peace years before with all that had happened, I was once again a bit surprised that no bitterness remained in my heart. Forgiveness had been the healing factor. The power of acceptance, of being cheerful, at peace, and content explains the smile on the face of an old man carrying the torch in a place where a young man had suffered the most.

# Remember Me
# This Way

★

*Louis in his early eighties. "I think my skateboarding*
*shakes up a few people. Some stop their cars*
*to be sure their eyes aren't deceiving them."*

# A Charitable Heart

If I had a time machine, all my memories, and could go back and live my life over, there's not too much I would change. Sure, maybe I wouldn't want to get on the Green Hornet and crash into the ocean, and drift, and be a POW, and have PTSD, and all the rest—but there's no use in speculating. It took that experience to get to where I am now: telling my story, doing charitable work, saving lives, giving counsel, and helping kids.

It's been a great life, especially working with the kids.

And now look at what's happened: I have two great books about me, the most beautiful woman in the world directing a movie about my life—and hugging me. I have a wonderful family, strong faith, and so many friends. Who can complain? I accept everything.

As I've always said: All things work together for good.

I'm 97 years old and, like everyone else, a little afraid of death because no matter how old you are you're always making plans and you don't want to be interrupted. I feel as if I've already lived two hundred years, but I wouldn't mind two hundred more just so I can keep doing what I've been doing: helping the underdog. That's been my program. That's been my whole life.

I'm a thankful citizen of America who just wants to be remembered for his charitable heart.

# Afterword

On July 13, 2014, eleven days after Louis Zamperini passed away at 97, the family held a private memorial to celebrate his life. Among the speakers: Louie's daughter, Cynthia; son, Luke; grandson, Clay; *60 Minutes* producer and long-time friend Draggan Mihailovich; Angelina Jolie; and Kyle Gauthier, whose reflections appeared earlier in the book. Each shared emotional memories of the man who had so enriched their lives.

## LUKE ZAMPERINI

Louis was prepared. When his plane crashed in the Pacific Ocean in 1943 he was prepared for the ordeal. As a Boy Scout, he learned that bullets lose velocity in about three to four feet of water. Studying physiology in college he learned that the mind was like a muscle. It would atrophy if not exercised. And taking a course offered to all troops in the Hawaiian

Islands—but only fifteen servicemen attended, he said—he learned how to deal with sharks in the water. Learning to drive from my father was not so much about operating the vehicle as it was a course in advance contingency planning.

Louis was funny. When my mother came home after traveling around the world by tramp steamer in the 1960s, she told us about walking up to the pyramids when a local man slapped her on the bottom. Dad asked, "What did you do?" She said, "I picked up a rock and threw it at him." Dad said, "You should have done the Christian thing and turned the other cheek."

In 1998, when asked by the mayor of Joetsu, Japan, if there was anything good about being in a Japanese prison camp, he answered quickly: "Yes. It prepared me for fifty-five years of married life."

Louis was loving. Like most of his generation, my dad expressed his love in acts of service. Later on in life he began to start saying, "I love you." But early on he showed his love by knowing that you had a need and then just doing something about it.

For instance, he didn't care much for the pet rats I had as a child, but one day after my carelessness seemingly caused their untimely end, my dad determined that they were still alive, and he stayed up all night feeding them sugar water from an eyedropper and nursing them back to health. In the morning I was surprised and excited beyond belief.

When I was older, he noticed that a tree was leaning dangerously on the roof of my house. He single-handedly removed it while I was at work.

Louis was miraculous. He didn't perform miracles to demonstrate his power before men, but miracles happened to him to demonstrate the power of God in his life. A few that come to mind was the miraculous escape from the crashed bomber after having been pinned under the waist gunner's tripod, wrapped in coiled cabling, and passing out as the plane sank, then coming to and floating free without any explanation. When a Japanese fighter strafed his raft with forty-eight bullet holes, none of the three occupants crammed into that tiny space was injured. In prison camp he held a heavy wooden plank over his head for thirty-seven minutes.

But the greatest miracle was finding reconciliation with his creator and then forgiving all those who had tormented him—including the Bird. Two years of recurring nightmares in which he throttled the Bird, over in an instant—and never to resume for the rest of his life.

Louis was my Dad, my hero, and my role model. I miss him greatly.

## DRAGGAN MIHAILOVICH

One day in 1999, Louie wanted to take me to his hometown of Torrance, a few exits south of LA, so that he could show me Zamperini Field, the airfield that had been named in his honor. The piece I'd done on Louie for the Winter Olympics had aired the year before, but we were friends now, and I made it a point to see him whenever I was in Los Angeles.

Louie was driving his Subaru wagon and I was a little nervous sitting in the passenger seat with an eighty-two-year-old at the wheel. But I figured if he could fly a plane, he could drive a car. The first thing I noticed is that Louie liked to sit really low and far back, his long legs stretched out.

We were negotiating the boulevards of Hollywood and Westwood, heading for the freeway, when suddenly an Audi came to an abrupt stop in front of us in the left lane. In an instant, my eyes widened, my heart skipped a beat, and I wondered if Louie was seeing what I was seeing. If not, we were about to have the four interlocked Audi logo circles permanently branded on our faces. Before I could gasp or find my voice, Louie swooshed the steering wheel sharply to the right, and then just as quickly swung the steering wheel to the left. He had evaded the Audi by darting cleanly into the center lane—and then back to our original path.

Holy smokes, I thought. That was impressive. Two seconds passed. Three. Another. Finally, Louie turned to me and quite matter-of-factly said, "I've still got it, don't I?"

Did he ever.

And he never lost it.

## CLAY ZAMPERINI

The loss of my grandfather has been difficult to process. It's not that I can't imagine a world without him in it, but rather that his passing is a loss that is not unique to my family, but affects an unfathomable number of people.

Louis Zamperini has been a lot of things to a lot of people: An example of elite athleticism and a reminder that with hard work and direction, we are all capable of anything. A testament to the strength and resilience of the human spirit when, despite his hopeless situation, he and Russell Philips survived a forty-seven-day-long journey lost at sea. Perhaps most important, he has been an example of our own ability to free ourselves from our demons when he forgave his prison guards for torturing him for two-and-a-half years.

But to me, he has always just been my grandfather. The loving, kind, and generous man who went above and beyond to give me a chance at a better life than he had, and the wisdom to be a better man than he was. That's a tough act to follow. Louis taught me what it is to be strong, what it is to be compassionate. He taught me that by holding on to anger and bitterness, I would only hurt myself. He often told me that the most important thing I should remember was to "have a cheerful countenance at all times." No matter how grim your situation is, whether you're lost at sea, or just having a bad day, keeping a positive, cheerful attitude is the key to your own survival.

I can only count it as a blessing that these lessons from the Greatest Generation, or what he called "the Hardy Generation," resonate not only with my generation, but with the countless other young people who have looked up to him as a beacon of wisdom and a life well lived. I am continually amazed to hear how many of my own friends held Louis in their own hearts. Given his love and concern for youth, it is no wonder.

I owe so much of my own identity to my grandfather. He was an adventurer and an outdoorsman, and he planted the seed for my own love of the wilderness, rock climbing, mountaineering, and taking time to stop and marvel in the glory of creation. In my own copy of *Unbroken*, Louis left me his signature and a quote from a man he admired, renowned environmentalist John Muir.

"Climb the mountains and get their good tidings. Nature's peace will flow into you as sunshine flows into trees. The winds will blow their own freshness into you, and the storms their energy, while cares will drop away from you like the leaves of Autumn."

## CYNTHIA ZAMPERINI GARRIS

I wrote this letter to my father on his 90th birthday.

*You saved my life when I was drowning in someone's pool long ago. You took care of me when I was sick. You* tenderly removed many a splinter from my feet, bandaged my every wound, and took me into your arms at night when I was afraid.

You taught me the value of honesty.

You inspired me to become a Christian when I was so young, and then I had both you and Jesus to make me feel safe and loved.

You had an athlete's dinner on the table for me night after night when I'd return from hours of ballet lessons. Years later you taught me to ski, thus beginning an even closer friendship between us.

You've taken me with you to Japan and the Marshall Islands, both wonderful adventures I'll always remember.

You've been my date for hundreds of lunches at El Cholo.

You continue to inspire me with your joyous spirit, enduring strength, unyielding health, and ability to land on your feet no matter what.

Last year both Luke and I found ourselves remarking that we wished we could be more like you: that you are healthier and happier than we have ever been, and that you have more friends than we could ever hope for.

What is it about you that is so very special? That kept you alive through the war? That helped you cheat death so many times in your life? That keeps you going through thick and thin, and that draws people by the hundreds to want to be with you?

*I was asked this question while being interviewed in Torrance yesterday and I couldn't put my finger on it. I've tried to figure it out in the past and still fall short of knowing. Maybe even you don't know.*

*All I know is that you have it and always will. That undying flame within you is one and the same with the Olympic flame. You are both forged together forever. You are that flame of inspiration to all that have come before, and to all that will ever be.*

*But most of all, in my most intimate heart, you're my friend, teacher, companion, and champion.*

*You're my dad.*

*And with all the love a daughter can express, I thank you for bringing me into this world so that I could know you.*

# Acknowledgments

## LOUIS ZAMPERINI

Whatever I have accomplished I owe to the sacrifices of my mother and father; to the support of my sisters Virginia and Sylvia; and especially the love of my brother, Pete, who convinced me to run and saved my life. He was my mentor and inspiration.

I also owe much to my late wife, Cynthia. We were partners in a fifty-five-year adventure called marriage. She knew me before and after I changed my life and stuck with me through all of it. Thanks to her love, influence, and persistence we accomplished more than I dreamed possible.

I'm always grateful to my children, Cissy and Luke, who stand by me without fail. Also, my grandson, Clayton; his mother, Lisa; and my son-in-law, Mick. Their love and support mean the world to me.

Author David Rensin, who collaborated with me on my

2003 autobiography, *Devil at My Heels*, once again captured my voice, plain and simple, and brought my story to life. Finding someone you can trust and work with day in and day out is the most precious thing. Thank you, David.

I'm indebted to producer Draggan Mihailovich, who "rediscovered" me and, through CBS Sports and the 1998 Winter Olympics at Nagano, Japan, most certainly resurrected me. Thanks to author Laura Hillenbrand, who found me while researching her book *Seabiscuit*, and just as I finished my story in my own words asked if she could be my biographer. Her unbreakable commitment and passion once again brought my story to the world.

Thanks to the student body and teachers of Torrance High School who cheered me on at the beginning of my athletic career, as well as the entire city of Torrance, and the local police who chased me up and down every street in town.

This book, as well as my previous books, is a tribute to the memory of our faithful B-24 crew who did not return alive. It is also in recognition of the many thousands of young people in school and camp programs to whom I've spoken across the nation, worked with, or counseled directly these past sixty years.

Thanks also to the Reverend Dr. Billy Graham for his message that caused me to turn my life around.

I'm grateful to my agent, Brian DeFiore, for going above

and beyond and then some, as well as my lawyer, Andrew Rigrod. Also, Peter Hubbard, Lynn Grady, and the entire team at Dey Street Books/HarperCollins, who believed in me immediately. My thanks also to Claudia Connal and everyone at Piatkus (Little, Brown) in the United Kingdom.

Finally, what can I say about the extraordinary Angelina Jolie? Her bravery, intelligence, and love in bringing my story to the big screen finally made the difference and brought a long-held dream of mine to life. Brad Pitt supported her every step of the way. Thanks also to Universal Pictures, who wanted to make this picture starting in 1957, and never gave up.

Of course, there are so many including Sophie Tedesco, Matt Baer, Ron Salisbury, Debbie Hayes, Robert Yonover, the Torrance Historical Society, and Jim Standifer, as well as others living and gone, who in ways large and small contributed to my life. Had I the space I would mention every name, but I'll take comfort that you and your families know who you are. Thank you all.

## DAVID RENSIN

For almost sixteen years I have had the greatest respect for Louie Zamperini. He lived a miraculous life, set an indelible and inspirational example, and has taught me more than I ever expected to learn. I'm so glad he decided that he still had something to say to the world, and the desire to complete our long-simmering project. All things do work together for good.

The devil may have been at Louie's heels, but Lucifer never caught him.

Thanks to my agent, Brian DeFiore, for always being open to my instincts, and then for making it possible for me to embark on yet another new adventure. As usual, Cynthia Price shared her eagle editorial eye, moral support, and grace under pressure: just three of the many reasons I have never done a book without her. For friendship, counsel, spadework, and ceaseless encouragement, I'm indebted to Bill Zehme, Joe Rensin and family, George Hodak, Nancy Rommelmann, Erika Schickel, Steve Randall, Amy Alkon, Zorianna Kit, Jennifer Gates, Eric Estrin, Mark Ebner, SA Jennifer Laurie, Lisa Kusel, Jane and Gary Peterson, Paul Peterson, Joshua Marquis, Samantha Dunn, Laurie Abkemeier, Carrie Ann Neeson, Taffy Brodesser-Akner, Aria Sheeks, Dennis Klein, Brandy Engler, Cheryl Bianchi, Mike Thomas, Sara Grace Cast, Bruce Kluger and Diana Price. Did I forget anyone? Apologies. If you think you should be in this list, then you absolutely are.

Cynthia Zamperini Garris, Mick Garris, and Luke and Lisa Zamperini were unstinting in their faith and trust. Thanks also to Draggan Mihailovich, Clay Zamperini, and Kyle Gauthier for sharing their precious memories.

Dey Street Books executive editor Peter Hubbard, publisher Lynn Grady, and their enthusiastic team led the way forward. Thanks also to Claudia Connal and the dedicated staff at Piatkus (Little, Brown) in the United Kingdom.

David Mackintosh contributed his excellent photo editing, and I'm grateful to the LA84 Foundation for their permission to quote from George Hodak's interview for the then-named Amateur Athletic Foundation of Los Angeles.

Finally, I wouldn't be part of this extraordinary experience were it not for the late Cynthia Zamperini, a friend since she acted as the intermediary between me and surfer Miki Dora for a magazine profile in 1982, and always urged him to do a book with me. When I finally did the book—*All for a Few Perfect Waves*—both Miki and Cynthia had passed away, but her restless spirit informs the result. Cynthia also introduced me to Louie and is responsible for our collaborations. I've always appreciated her lust for life and certainty that I could tell Louie's story. I miss her unique and delightful voice.

As always all my love and gratitude in great measure for my wife, Suzie Peterson, and our son, Emmett Rensin—now an excellent writer himself. (He makes me beyond proud.) Their support, indulgence, wisdom, and willingness to put up for years with a guy who's gone to great lengths to avoid ever having a regular job make all things possible. People may tell me everything but you both mean everything to me.

Input about this book and *Devil at My Heels* is welcome at my website, http://www.tellmeeverything.com/tellme.html, and encouraged in the comment and review sections of all online bookstores, news media, and social networks. We'd love to hear what you think. Thanks!

Former Olympian and World War II POW who survived 47 days on a raft in the Pacific Ocean, **Louis Zamperini,** is the hero of Laura Hillenbrand's 2010 international bestseller *Unbroken*. The film based on that book will be released at Christmas 2014 (directed by Angelina Jolie). In 2003 Louis wrote his own widely-read autobiography, *Devil At My Heels*. He died in July 2014 at age 97.

**David Rensin** has authored and co-authored 16 books, including *The Mailroom: Hollywood History from the Bottom Up* and *All For a Few Perfect Waves*, about rebel surfer Miki Dora. He also helped Louis Zamperini write *Devil at My Heels*.